Buddhist Psychology

Buddhist Psychology

An Inquiry into the Analysis and Theory of Mind in Pālī Literature

C.A.F. Rhys Davids

DEV PUBLISHERS & DISTRIBUTORS
New Delhi

Published by:
Dev Publishers & Distributors
2nd Floor, Prakash Deep,
22, Delhi Medical Association Road,
Darya Ganj,w
New Delhi-110002
Phone : 011-43572647
e-mail: devbooks@hotmail.com
website: www.devbooks.co.in

ISBN 978-93-81406-10-6
This edition 2012

Printed in India

Contents

Preface

My book is an atternpt to envisage faithfully something true in the history of a very interesting current in human ideas. This 'something true' is the analysis and theory of mind in the movement and culture we understand by Early Buddhism, as well as in that of its direct descendant still thriving in Burma, Ceylon and Siam, called Theravāda, or the Doctrine of the Elders. This also is called Buddhism—some call it Hīna-Yāna, some Southern Buddhism.

As to the book's quests and goals, two of the more proximate may suffice. While scholars are beginning to get at and decipher the long-buried treasure of Buddhist writings brought from Mid-Asia, the general reader is being told that the group of other descendants from Early Buddhism called Mahā-Yānism, is not only evolved from the earlier doctrine, but is its completion and apotheosis. The reader cannot judge in this matter, unless he has an all-round knowledge of what the developed system started from. Such a knowledge is not always present in those who are fluent about the complete descendant. Henee he is placed in the position of one who learns of Neo-Platonism and not of Plato, of Aquinas and not of Aristotle. My book's quest is to present summarily some of the thought contained in the mother-doctrine and her first-born child, much of which is still inaccessible to him.

The second object is to bring nearer the day when the historical treatment of psychology will find it impossible to pretend that the observation and analysis of mind began with the Pre-Socratics. Psychologists are, some of them, curiously unhistorical, even with regard to the European field with its high fence of ignorance and prejudice. Theories are sometimes put forward as new that have been anticipated in both Europe and Asia. I say 'curiously,' because the history of ideas about the mind is both fascinating and suggestive. Would Professor Bergson say of his brother thinkers, too, especially of the more constructive among them (I dare to include himself), that the past of psychological thought also *est là, continuellement,* but that so intent is their forward gaze that they 'cannot and must not look back'? Yet how much more impressive might they not make the present for us if they would, if they felt compelled to look back a little more! Let us hope that monographs in psychological history may eventually succeed in making it unecessary for frowing, or other catastrophes, to bring flooding in upon them the ignored past of ideas in Indian philosophy.

With so large an object in so small a book, it has been impossible to compare the line of descent I have chosen with other lines, even with that of the Mādhyamika school, in which Professor de la Vallée Poussin has revealed much interesting psychological matter. I have also to apologize for bringing in severl terms in the original. This was as inevitable, for clearness and unambiguity, as would be the use of corresponding Greek words in writing on Greek psychology. But we are more used to Greek words. Finally, if I have repeated statements made in previous writings, it was to avoid irritating the reader by too many references, as if suggesting that he might as well be reading not one book, but three or four.

C.A.F. Rhys Davids

February 1914

1

Habits of Thought

There are some to-day who say that enough is known of 'Buddhism,' by the portions of its literature translated into English and German, to enable anyone to form correct judgments concerning the data and conclusions grouped under that term, without further acquaintance with that literature at second hand, let alone at first hand.

This is a fairly tenable view if by Buddhism be meant just a certain ethical reform movement, a gospel set on foot to save souls and roll back the murk of sin and superstition, a new creed with a revived moral code. But when we gain a wider perspective of Buddhism, and look more deeply into what is involved by the term, we may feel less confident. Buddhism really covers the thought and culture of a great part of India for some centuries, as well as that of Further India (*pace* China and Japan), up till the present. And the reader of translations from its literature, be he superficial or thoughtful, is bound to come across strange things in the point of view, the values, the logic, which should make him realize that the Semitic and Hellenic stock on which his own religious and philosophic principles are grafted, does not coincide with that from which the traditional notions revealed in Buddhism have sprung.

Now if our knowledge of the notions at the heart of Greek and Roman culture and religion has recently been most notably deepened and clarified by research in a literature which has been long in our hands, how much may we not yet have to learn of the history of other human ideas, the literature expressing which is but partly accessible not only to readers of translations, but even to investigators of the original texts?

To write on the subject of this book with the authority of a master, would imply a familiarity, not only with certain works of the Buddhist canonical books, mostly as yet untranslated, but also with the elaborations in theory made by the great scholastics, none of which are translated, and but a few of which are yet printed. Hence this rough provisional sketch can but serve as a temporary makeshift, born of half-knowledge, till in another decade of this century some writer, better equipped in every way, is able adequately to deal with it.

For even in the original cult and school of Buddhism, known as Hīna-Yāna, or better as Theravāda—the Doctrine of the Elders—maintained down to the present in Further India, it is true of its psychology, even more perhaps than of any other branch of learning, that we have here no body of knowledge evolved in a night to be clothed forthwith in a nutshell. It reveals a growth as does the psychology of Europe, which evolved from the *De Anima* of Aristotle to the *Méditations*, and the rest, of Cartesianism. Compared with the latter evolution, the psychology of the Theravāda is as a quiet river, flowing often unseen, compared to a stream torn by cataracts. There are in it no ruptures of an ecclesiasticism replacing 'paganism,' and so forth. It is probable—and it certainly pleases our pride to think so—that no quiet consistent internal growth can produce such notable results as have come from our own more cataclysmic struggles out of barbarism and superstition into relatively free and developed analysis of mind. However that may be, the historian of Buddhist psychology has a growth to discern and describe, from its earliest recorded expressions in the Suttanta, or books of Suttas, again in the analytical works known as Abhidhamma-Piṭaka, and other early surviving books, down to the discursive commentaries of the present era, the work of eminent scholastics.

We shall hardly expect to find, in any of these classic works, that detached and specialized study of mental life as such, which under its modern name of psychology is a matter of yesterday among ourselves. From Aristotle to Hamilton and J.S. Mill, scientific analysis of mind has been discussed either incidentally in philosophic subject-matter, or as the leading subject, but with incursions into the field of metaphysic and ethics. These are also the methods we find in Buddhist inquiries into the nature and processes of mind. If we take up the mediaeval classic compendium of philosophy and psychology, recently made accessible to English readers—Anuruddha's *Abhidhammattha-sangaha*[1]—we find, here a notable analysis of cognition sandwiched between metaphysical statements, and there an examination of states of consciousness complicated by ethical considerations.

Hence it will be necessary to dig out and excise our materials from their context. And in noting the results, the reader cannot be too careful to mark whether they are yielded by the older literary strata, or by earlier or later scholastic work discussing those older canonical scriptures. The materials are not yet ready for dealing properly with the scholastic psychology as a rounded-off body of doctrine. I am rather presenting the subject in approximately Buddhist fashion; the older matter as justifying, and illustrated by, the later expositions. And I am not seldom poaching in philosophical preserves.

Since, however, the Compendium, or digest just referred to, is the only text yet published giving a purview of Buddhist philosophy of life and mind, a glance at its point of departure may attune our own understanding to a difference in scale of contents and of values from that which is habitual to us. In true thought are no 'habits of thought,' writes Mr. Fielding-Hall, in his enthralling book *The Passing of Empire*. That is so ideally, but actually all thinking is only relatively true; for *all* thinking has been and is done by way of habits, that is, traditions, of thought. Vast is the fleeting show of the world, and brief the current of each span of life. We must economize in methods of thought, and this can only be done by following the beaten tracks of our own traditional methods, when we assimilate new perceptions to establish generalizations.

But there are beaten tracks other than ours, habits of thought not European, along which philosophizing was flowing before 'we' began, and still flows. And our difficulties in understanding those philosophies lie less in learning the results, than in getting out of our own beaten groove into the 'habit of thought' along which those results were come at.

The Compendium starts with assuming four categories of ultimate notions: *not* the One and the Many, *not* the Real and the Ideal, but (1) *chitta*,[2] consciousness (mind, 'heart,' intelligence); (2) *chetasikā* (literally, mental things, mentals); (3) *rūpa* (literally, shape, visible form, material quality); (4) *nibbāna* (*nirvāṇa*, or *summum bonum*). Roughly speaking, we may approximate these to our own ultimates: (1 and 2) mind or consciousness; (3) matter; (4) happiness, or the ideal. But it is, I repeat, a rough, an approximate fit only; our logic kicks against finding a co-ordination, as ultimates, of (1) consciousness, and (2) phases or factors of consciousness. Nor are we content to substitute for a purely spiritual, negatively expressed concept our own more comprehensive and more positively conceived terms for the *summum bonum.* We shall probably conclude that we here see a section of humanity beating out its way to truth along lines that are parallel to, or even convergent with our own, but different—different in its point of departure, different in its intervening experiences, different in its 'habits of thought.'

But the fact that these categories start, not with abstract generalizations such as unity, plurality, reality, substance, but with consciousness and, so to speak, coefficients of consciousness, should certainly bring us to this conclusion, if to none other, namely, that such a view argues *a very close attention bestowed on the nature and work of mind.* The output of that attention it is my business presently to summarize. Two points, before we leave the Compendium to dig in the older books, may serve to bring out that difference of standpoint in this old Eastern, if mainly Aryan, view of things.

The next step in the manual brings us up against a vastness in extension assigned to *chitta* undreamt of by ourselves when we set out to analyze consciousness. *Chitta*, we read, is fourfold, according as it is experienced in one of the three *loka's*, or planes of life, or, fourthly, by one who, for the time being, is 'beyond-a-*loka*' (*lōk'-uttara*) as to his thought. These three *loka*'s include the whole universe of being, from creatures infra-human up to both the inferior celestial worlds and the superior—a purview greatly exceeding, if parallel to that of Aquinas, who confines himself to discussion on the consciousness of 'the angels' only. He includes an analysis of the angelic nature to complete his scheme of *formoe separatoe.* Buddhism has always held that, by dint of sedulous practice in prescribed forms of contemplative exercise, mundane consciousness might be temporarily transformed into the consciousness experienced in either the less material, or the quite immaterial worlds. It has therefore both Aquinas's reason and this too for its fourfold scheme of *chitta.*

Mr. Aung, as an 'interpreter of . . . mediaeval Buddhism presented through modern Burmese glasses,'[3] figures *chitta* and *chetasika's* as the shell and the contents of a sphere,[4] and shows, both hereby and by the context, that this tradition is content to envisage the two concepts as respectively a whole and its factors, or else as respectively a unity 'and something more,' 'concomitant' with that unity. And thus some among us will still be left chafing at the logic of four categories which should be three.

The rest of us will suspend our judgment and get on, bearing two things in mind as we do so. Firstly, that our traditional logic of whole and parts, genus and species, is a convenient Greek fiction, by which we artificially parcel off the flow or *continuum* of experience as if we were sorting seeds or the like. It is a mental instrument which plays a relatively minor part in Indian thought. When the Aristotelian and his heirs divide the knowable into bundles, and sub-bundles, ranging the individual everywhere under the more general, the Buddhist thinker, especially in the philosophy of mind, saw everywhere confluences, conjunctures of conditions and tendencies, from which at a given *locus* (*ṭhāna, okāsa*) something individual came to pass. He stood for the emergence of the Particular; the Greek, for the revelation of the Universal.

But let this not be strained. Buddhist thought is very largely an inquiry into mind and its activities. Now in that field, as an eminent psychologist has observed,[5] "a difference in aspects is a difference in things." For the 'things' or subject-matter of psychology are the aspects under which things present themselves to mind. Hence we can find it natural enough for psychological philosophers to see, as psychologically, if not as logically, distinguishable categories: (1) the aspect of a sensitive, reacting, discrim inating consciousness *happening* in living individuals; and (2) the aspect of an ever-varying confluence of co-efficient mental complexes, evoked along with the ever-recurring, bare happening of that consciousness.

Taking one further glance at the Compendium before we shut the book, we are again repelled by an analysis of consciousness as immoral and as moral, *i.e.* as bad and as good, ethically speaking. We have learnt, in modern text-books, that ethical considerations are to be kept severely apart from what is held to be scientific investigation of facts, mental or other, of things as they are or appear to be. Those considerations deal with the 'ought to be,' and why.

Here again we come upon a difference of 'habit of thought.' For the Buddhist, the ethical goodness or badness of a state of consciousness was a primary quality of that consciousness no less than, for us, extension and solidity are reckoned as primary qualities of external things, accessible to touch. 'There is nothing good but thinking makes it so' was never a Buddhist dictum. You act, speak, think, say, in a good way, whatever you or others may think about it. 'A good, moral, or meritorious act' means that a desirable result will follow such an act, sooner or later, inevitably. And an opposite sort of result will follow no less the opposite sort of act. The doing will entail suffering. These opposed qualities are integral parts of the content of mental activity, wrought up in its texture. They are, therefore, not out of place in an analysis of consciousness, and I doubt if even at this time of day a Buddhist, writing on psychology, would judge that such considerations involved trespass outside his legitimate range.

With these remarks on some of the differences in the point of view between the Buddhist outlook and that of our own tradition, we pass on to survey some of the older judgments concerning mind and consciousness. We shall not fail to find many of these judgments on all fours with our own stock of conceptions. But the different avenues along which the Indian mind has travelled are always more or less patent. Hence the difficulty found by both readers and writers in looking at the things of life and mind with Buddhist eyes, and hence the many mistakes we commit.

References

1. Translated as *A Compendium of Philosophy* (see Bibliography).
2. More strictly transliterated *citta;* but so spelt throughout to ensure correct pronunciation, as in our word *chit.* Both the *t*'s should be pronounced: *chit-ta.*
3. *Compendium,* p. 284.
4. *Ibid.* p. 13.
5. James Ward, *Ency. Brit.,* art. 'Psychology.'

2

The Psychology of the Nikāyas

I. Mind in term and Concept

Psychological material is never far to seek in Buddhist books, unless their subject-matter mainly precludes such a content. This is the case with the first of the canonical Piṭakas, the Vinaya, the subject of which is, for the most part, the organization and rules of the Sangha, or fraternity of men and women 'in orders.' In the following four collections of Suttas, or discourses, entitled the Nikāyas, which correspond in authority and sanctity to the Gospels and Epistles of the Christian Scriptures, there is more or less matter of psychological interest in each of the four; the third Nikāya, called Saṃyutta, contains on the whole the most. Five of its parts are ostensibly concerned with the mental and physical constituents of the individual, with sense (organ and object of sense), with feeling, and with purpose. In the fifth Nikāya—a miscellaneous group of books—the psychological matter is almost always incidental. Generally, the high ethical or spiritual importance of grasping aright the nature of mind, or mental process, is affirmed. And in a Sutta of the second Nikāya, the founder of Buddhism is represented as betraying himself to an adherent, who had never before seen him, by a discourse largely on the nature of mind.[1]

What were the reasons for this emphasis? Chiefly two: the one theoretical, the other ethical.[2]

(1) Apparently because consciousness or mind was judged

to be the most striking, the most typical, the most conclusive instance of that perpetual movement, change, happening-and-ceasing in the nature of everything which was summed up chiefly in the word 'impermanent.'[3] To body, when not regarded molecularly, a relative permanence might be assigned, whether it were a human body or an elephant's, a tree or a mountain. But mind was conceived from the outset as a series of transient, if connected, happenings. And each momentary happening comprised three phases: a genetic, a static and an evanishing phase. So that, as the type of the impermanent, mind was different even at each fraction of its momentary duration:

"Better were it, bhikkhus, that the uneducated many-folk should conceive this four-element-made body, rather than chitta, *to be soul. And why? The body is seen to persist for a year, for two, three, Jour, five, ten or twenty years, for a generation. . . even for a hundred years, or even for longer, while that which is called consciousness, that is, mind, that is, intelligence, arises as one thing, ceases as another, both by night and by day."*[4]

This view is not that of substantialist philosophy—that is to say, it does not envisage *chitta* as an entity, persisting as the same during life, and *modified* constantly by external stimuli and inherent change. It is that of a series of phenomena, flash-points, we might call them, of intelligence, cinema-films, thaumatrope-figures, welded into an apparent unity, such as is brought about by these inventions. And they are welded *only thus far* into a phenomenal genuine unity, in that each moment of consciousness is causally connected, so long as each series lasts, with its predecessor.

There are no passages in the Nikāyas expounding *chitta* in terms of momentary *chittāni*, or consciousnesses. But it was inevitable that later exegesis would so develop the theme. And so it has been developed, and so developed, it is taught even at the present day, as we shall see later. But the Suttas elsewhere confirm the citation given above by another discourse, in which consciousness or mind is declared to be an intermittent manifestation, 'happening' only in reaction to a suitable stimulus, and ceasing when the stimulus was exhausted. As we might phrase it, mind in the individual organism was, in the absence of the requisite conditions for evoking it, only potential.

A bhikkhu, Sāti Fisher-son,[5] gives out as the Buddha's own teaching that "it is mind (*viññāṇa*) which persists and is reborn after death unchanged." He is summoned to repeat this before the Master. "Is it true, Sāti, that you said this?" "Yea, lord, so do, I understand you to teach." "What, Sāti, is this mind?" "That speaker, that feeler, lord, who experiences the result of good and evil deeds done here or there." "Now then, foolish man, whence got you such a doctrine as being teaching of mine? Have I not taught you by many methods that mind arises from a cause; and except from a cause, mind cannot come to be?"

The bhikkhus bear him out in this. He goes on :

> *"And consciousness is designated only in accordance with the condition causing it: visual consciousness from, the seeing eye and the seen object; auditory consciousness from the hearing ear and the sound; . . . thought from mind and mental object. Just as a fire is different according to the kind of fuel . . . . Do ye see, bhikkhus, that this is [something that has] beconme? Do ye see that the becoming is according to the stimulus* [lit. *food*] *? Do ye see that if the stimulus ceases, then that which has become ceases?"*

These two passages contain the whole of the Buddhist theory of mind or consciousness in the germ :—intermittent series of psychic throbs associated with a living organism beating out their coming-to-know through one brief span of life. The fact of those conscious pulsations, the category of these phenomena, conventionally expressed as a unity, as *chitta*, is accepted, both early and late, as an ultimate of experience, as an irreducible datum, not to be defined in terms of anything else.

There does not seem to have existed any inquiry into the fact and process of electricity, in early Indian thought, either for practical or for academic purposes, through which, as in our own philosophic evolution, the concepts of the ultimates in nature, in mind, might have been modified and developed. Yet the Buddhist conception of consciousness is, I venture to think, better understood as a mental electrification of the organism, than in terms of any other natural force or other phenomenon. The philosophic in-quirer, if European, is more likely to draw a comparison with Aristotle's principle of form or actualizing essence, which in the case of a living body 'informs' or 'entelechizes' matter, and without which that body has merely a 'potential' being. Consciousness, '*psyche*' or *chitta*, is the entelechy of the body, a psychically innervating force. Danger of fallacious confusion may, however, arise in any parallel drawn between even the modified noumenon of Aristotelian 'form' with the phenomenal Buddhist *chitta* or *viññāṇa*. 'Potential' applies rather to future *chittas* than to the material basis of the body. And in its highest manifestat-ion as *psychē*, Aristotle's 'form' becomes *noūs*, the *noūs poiētikos* which is held to be both perduring and immortal and 'from without,' 'alone divine.' None of these terms is ever applied to the Buddhist concept of mind.

Let us therefore abstain from such comparisons, and consider further the varying context in which the terms for that concept occur.

In the former citation from the Nikāyas, (pp.13*f.*) the three terms '*consciousness, that is, mind, that is, intelligence,*' are stated as mutually equivalent:

"cittaṃ iti pi mano it'i pi viññāṇaṃ."

In commenting, centuries later, on this passage, Buddhaghosa, the greatest of the scholastics, calls all three a name for the *manayatana*, or 'sphere of cognition.' Elsewhere the first two of the three terms are used as practically coincident,[6] but this is the only passage known to me where all three are so represented. This is no small comfort to the inquirer, for in referring, in the most general terms, to the phenomenon of mind or consciousness, the Nikāyas show a certain predilection for one term or other of the three according to the aspect under which that phenomenon is being discussed. And, in our ignorance of the stock of current nomenclature of which the Nikāyas made use, this predilection appears as somewhat arbitrary. It is therefore, I repeat, a good thing to know that it does not really matter which of the three terms is used; the meaning is practically identical.

For instance, when kinds of irreducible data are classified under the category *dhātu*—usually translated 'element'—we find the second and third terms of these three synonyms called *dhātu,* but never, I believe, the first of them (*chitta*). Earth, water, fire, air are grouped as 'elements,' in India as in Europe, and sometimes space is added, and sometimes consciousness (*viññāṇa-dhgātu*). Now the philosophic exegesis of the Commentaries considers the first four elements and consciousness not as substances, but rather as elemental irreducible data, as phenomenal, yet not unreal, as forces of momentary duration but infinitely recurring, and combining to form apparently persisting, apparently static 'things.' Thus earth stands for extended element, known by hardness (we should perhaps say 'solidity'), water stands for cohesive element, binding everything, fire stands for heat, air, for mobile element, while *viññāṇa* is the aware, or intelligent, element.

Again, to *mano* as prefixed to *dhātu* (and also to the dual compound, *mano-viññāṇa-dhātu*) is assigned a special function in consciousness, with which we can better deal later. Without these affixes *mano* may form the generic term for those functions; and it is also so used when its work is considered under the aspect of product, or karma, namely, in the phrase equivalent to our *'thought,* word and deed.' The Commentators connect *mano* with *mināti* (*mā*), to measure. And it is more usual, when the intellectual functioning of consciousness is referred to, to employ *mano*; *viññāṇa* representing the field of sense, and sense-reaction, and *chitta* standing pre-eminently for the subjective, inward-looking aspect of consciousness, conveyed by our lapsed word 'inwyt.'

When, however, the doctrine bears upon the psychology, or eschatology, of rebirth, with all the near-lurking notions of animistic transmigration, then the term for consciousness is usualy *viññāṇa,* never *mano. Chitta* appears only in the post-Nikāyan phrases: rebirth-*chitta* and decease-*chitta.* It must be remembered that Buddhists did not invent their terms for mind, etc., nor divert their current usage as to form and context. They only sought to infuse these terms that they found, with diverted meaning, like old bottles filled, with new wine. And we may safely conclude, from such discourses as that on Sāti's error, and from others involving legendary diction, that *viññāṇa* was the current and standard expression for that factor of the organism, which was commonly supposed alone to survive bodily dissolution, and to transmigrate, as the 'vehicle' of the soul. An analogous case would be that of an English divine or journalist discussing this factor in terms of 'mind,' or 'consciousness,' so long as the activities of this life were his subject, but substituting 'soul' when adverting to death and to consciousness after death. While for ignorant folk, from early Buddhist days down to the Burmese peasant of to-day, *viññāṇa* (or its Burmese equivalent) is conceived as the manifestation of soul (*attā*), that is, of a ghostly semi-material mannikin.

Among the Māra or Satanic folklore, which got wrought up into the more adult discussions of the Suttas, is the legend of Māra, the spirit of sensuous seduction, of the craving that involves dyings and rebirths, lurking around a death-bed, in the visible shape of murky 'smokiness,' looking for the escaping *viññāṇa* of the dying person. The legend is told twice in connection with the death of saintly bhikkhus, in whom *viññāṇa* was ceasing utterly to arise, because they had attained the end of life, earthly or celestial.[7] It belongs to the edifying literature of the Sutta-Piṭaka, and would be as out of place in a Buddhist philosophical discussion as it would be to write, in an examination paper on electrical physics, of a thunderbolt falling upon anybody. It was the popular way there and elsewhere, then and more or less always, to speak of a something flitting at death, perceptible perhaps only to vision not of men, at least of ordinary men. And the current term for the flitter, or flitting thing happening, in Kosala and Magadha, to be *viññāṇa,* Buddhist teaching, while seeking to correct the current notion, retained this word, when it might, equally well have used *chitta* or *mano.*

Again, the' genesis of intelligence in the human embryo is expressed by the use of *viññāṇa:*

"Were viññāṇa, *Ananda, not to descend into the mother's womb, would body and mind become constituted therein?"*[8]

It is doubtless another case of folklore speech accepted by the Suttanta teaching that the usual verb for happening or coming to be—viz. *uppajjati, uppatti,* arising or attaining—is here replaced by *avakkanti,* descent, a figure of speech more rare, though it is found in such phrases as 'descent of pain,' or 'of happiness.'[9]

For Buddhists the dissolution of the factors of a living individual at death was complete: body 'broke up' and mind or the incorporeal ceased. But if, in the final flickerings of mind or *vuññāṇa,* there was a coefficient of the desire to enjoy, involving a clinging to, or grasping after life wherewith to enjoy, then those dying pulsations, as cause or condition, *produced their effect,* not in the corpse, but in some embryo wakening elsewhere at that moment to life, it might be in the next house, it might be in some heaven, or purgatory.

"To him, bhikkhus, who lives intent on enjoyment in things that tend to enfetter us, there will be descent of vuññāṇa . . . *and where* viññāṇa *gains a footing, there is descent of mental and bodily life. . . for this nutriment,* viññāṇa, *is the cause of our taking birth, and coming again to be."*[10]

In the term translated above 'mental and bodily life'—*nāmarūpa,* literally, name and visible or material object, or form—we have yet another word annexed by Buddhism from current and traditional usage. It appears in the Brāhmaṇas, in what are presumably the pre-Buddhistic Upanishads, and in the Atharva-Veda, as a dual designation for the perishable and the imperishable factors of the individual. The Buddhist scholastics derive *nāma* exegetically from a root meaning 'to bend,' to emphasize the ductability of mind. But the ancient labelling of mind or soul by 'name' derives from a widespread feature of primitive culture, which sees, in the name, a status and a *raison d'être* for the individual over against the mystery and menace of a mainly hostile universe.

In the works just named, *nāma* and *rūpa* are, the two great manifestations—Word and Mind—of creative being or Brahman, as which 'It' descends into sky and earth.[11] And as *Sat,* Being, it permeates seed, egg, foetus, and 'spreads asunder' mortal *nāma*'s and *rūpa*'s in space.[12] In one passage it is they that are real, or actual, covering the immortal breath within them; in another, *nāma* appears as the immortal, leaving *rūpa* at death for infinite worlds.[13]

Buddhist thought—and herein it is, as ancient thought, so impressive—repudiated the Vedic and Vedāntist cosmology, although it suffered the borrowed word. It had no use for the faith and fantasy, which found satisfaction in perpetuating and elaborating primitive sagas about a world, for which a beginning and a creative agent were postulated. But there were the corporeal and incorporeal aspects of life to be accounted for, if not in their beginning, at least in their procedure and tendency. And this traditional term of *nāmarūpa* fitted them thus far, that it indicated the mental and bodily compound in the individual—a desideratum, this, in our own nomenclature.

In welding together a number of terms and categories drawn in part, doubtless, from current use, the compilers of the early Buddhist records have no more reduced their formulas to a flawless consistency than had the compilers of the Upanishads, to name no other scriptures. Thus *nāma* is not only (when joined with *rūpa*) not made synonymous with *chitta*, *viññāṇa* or *mano*; it is defined either as feeling, perceiving *viññāṇa*, and all complexes of thought, word and deed,[14] *or*, again, as the first two, and as volition, contact and attention.[15] The inconsistency is, however, more formal than real, since among those 'complexes' (whereof more presently), 'volition' and 'contact' are ranked foremost, 'attention' only coming into similar status in later psychology.[16] In the formula of Causal Genesis, or law of causation applied to life, *nāmarūpa* is not defined in terms of *viññāṇa*, because the former term serves to denote the newly reborn or reconceived human unit, while *viññāṇa* figures as the conditioning process, one *viññāṇa* being causal in the dying unit, another *viññāṇa* being caused in the embryonic unit. There was therefore a distinction in time, hence a distinction is made in definition.

Viññāṇa does not produce *nāmarūpa*, but because there is a functioning of the former as one span of life ends, a resultant functioning of fresh *viññāṇa* associated with a new *rūpa*, starts a fresh *nāmarūpa*. So might a man, murdered as he called for help on the telephone, have set going elsewhere, by his last words, a whole series of actions. We may call this transmitting a message, but we know not the nature of the electric force released, though we can say something about the medium for its transmission. We reckon on the force without speculating about it. We accept the transmission of mental qualities from parent to offspring without understanding it, and biological mathematicians now try to measure it, as electricity is measured. Some of us are inclined to discern here and there an analogous force in thought-transference or telepathy, albeit we do not understand its nature, or detect a medium of transference. Buddhists are equally unenlightened as to the nature and medium of the re-birth-force, but for them its logic is irrefutable. And whereas the vast field of possible antecedents for any individual rebirth make scientific inquiry fairly bootless, the theory does not break its shins, as does our theory of heredity, against the anomalies arising in the transmission of mental faculties, the conditions of which are yet unsolved by science.

One more term for consciousness, in addition to these four,—*chitta, mano, viññāṇa, nāma,*—refers us to the aspect of mind known in our psychology as consciousness of self, or presentation of the self, or ego, Pali *attā* (Sansk. *ātman*). Joined to *bhāva*, state, *attabhāva* is a useful term for personality, individuality.

> *"I, sir, during the time I have had experience through this* attabhāva, *am not capable of remembering what have been its characteristics and habits; how then should I remember former existences?"*[17]

The word includes the entire living human compound in any one span of life. And its use was judged to be, if necessary, not always harmless. "The body and the mental constituents are here," runs Buddhaghosa's exegesis on another context, "termed *attabhāva*, after the usage of average folk who say: 'This is my self.'"[18] Even without the affix, the word is used, though rarely, in the sense of personal appearance. Thus in the *Questions of King Milinda*: "But given mirror, light and face opposite, there would be [one's] self (*attā*)."[19] Usually, however, in the older books perhaps invariably, it is only in the oblique cases that *attā* is employed in a parallel sense to our reflexive pronoun. It is only in the nominative case, speaking approximately, that it acquires psychological emphasis as the representative and re-representative concept of a *subject* of mental objects, of conscious presentations and representations—a concept harmless enough as a necessary economical fiction of thought and speech, but deemed a very jungle of error for the man in the street.

Legitimately used in this form, it may function (*a*) like our term 'conscience,' *i.e.* moral consciousness—

> *"Does the self reproach thee not as to virtue?"*[20]
> *"The self, O man, knows thee as truthful or as false."*[21]
> *"The self well tamed is man's true sacrificial fire."*[22]

(this meaning is also found in oblique cases [23])—or (*b*) in the work of introspection generally:

"In so far as a bhikkhu knows the self (or himself, attānaṃ) *to this effect: 'thus far am I in faith, morals, learning, self-surrender, insight, ready speech,' —he is called knower of self* (attaññū)."[24]

The conlplement to this on the side of action is :

"a bkikkhn who without deceit or guile manifests the self (himself) as he really is."[25]

An interesting feature in some of these attempts at self-expression, for which all languages seem to prove very inadequate instruments, is the bifurcated or dual self. We see here, as in other literatures, the notion of one's self and another self dramatizing, so to speak, amongst the flow of individual subjective experience, and resolving the one self into plurality:

"These are the penalties of wrong-doing: the self upbraids self . . ."[26]

"Any virtuous layman established in the fourfold peace [of religious faith] can, if he will, confess himself to himself as assured of happy rebirth, and as having enlightenment as his final goal."[27]

"To whom is the self not dear? To evil-doers, for. . . though they may say 'Dear to us is the self,' yet that which a man disliked would do to one disliked, that do they by the self to the self."[28]

"By self incite the self examine self
By self, self-guarded thus, watchful of mind
And happy shalt thou live. For self of self
Is warder, unto self hath self recourse.
Therefore train well thyself, as'twere a steed
Well bred by trainer for the market reared."[29]

This dual mental projection is at times expressed by *chitta* and the closely allied term *cheto,* as if we should speak of mind affecting will, or 'heart' influencing 'head:'

"Ye should restrain, curb, subdue chitta *by* cheto. . . ."[30]

But this is a very rare variant, usually reserved for the *cheto* of one person discerning, 'reading,' as we say, the 'thought' (*cheto, chitta*) of another; whereof more presently.

That this mental fiction of self presented to self, as of a

lower to a 'higher self,' as we say,—this quasi-personification of alternating phases in the mental *continua*, one set of judgments and values jostling on another,—was considered by the scholastics as mere phraseological method, is shown by the passing over of such expressions, in their painstaking exegeses, without comment.

The *an-attā* position in the Nikāyas cannot be properly judged by those who are acquainted only with the European conception of 'souls.' These pathetic creations—the little fluttering sprites on Greek vases, the melancholy shades in Vergil's, later, in Dante's, other-world, or -worlds, the errant, fallible, doubled self which we meet with in mediaeval literature, the

> *"Animula vagula blandula*
> *Pallidula rigida nudula"*

of Hadrian—the Buddha might conceivably have classed as a sixth group in the organism. But whereas such notions are not absent from the early literature of India, the anti-*attā* argument of Buddhism is mainly and consistently directed against the notion of a soul, which was not only a persistent, unchanging, blissful, transmigrating, superphenomenal being, but was also a being wherein the supreme Ātman or world-soul was immanent, one with it in essence, and, as a bodily or mental factor, issuing its fiat.'[31] This theory, so prominent in the Upanishads, is evidently alluded, to in the second discourse ascribed to the Buddha:

"The body. . . [and so on for mental factors] . . . *is not the Self. If it were the Self, the body would not be subject to disease, and we should be able to say: "Let my body (or mind) be such and such a one, let my body not be such and such a one!' But since the body is not the Self, therefore it is subject to disease, and we are not able to say: 'Let, etc.' Now of that which is perishable, liable to suffering, subject to change, is it possible so to regard it as to say: This is of Me; this am I, this is the Self (soul) of me?"*[32]

I venture to think that this argument would never have

suggested itself to a European pluralist or phenomenalist. He would not associate omnipotence or bliss, as well as immortal continuity, with soul or ego. But however the entity was conceived, the main ground of its rejection in Buddhism was its supposed exemption from the universal laws of causation, ill and impermanence.

Whether that entity was called *satta* (being), *attā, jīva* (living principle) or *puggala* (person) did not matter:

"For these are merely names, expressions, turns of speech, designations in common use in the world. Of these he who has won truth makes use indeed, but is not led astray by them."[33]

And Buddhist doctrine never hesitates, as we have seen, to make use of customary phrases as a medium of exposition. The Suttas represent, for the most part, the effort of mature, cultured minds reaching out to guide immature, less cultured minds. The phrases and standpoints, useful for that purpose, cease to be used when the more academic method of set and general formulas called Abhidhamma is observed. When teaching is by way of that method, we no longer hear of a Self A discerning, judging, controlling self B, self C and so forth. All is then in terms of process, genesis, causation, series, and mental data, states or phenomena (*dhammā*). Now the *attā*, as popularly and as theologically conceived, was an entity distinct from phenomena, a self-existent something that 'perdured' while they arose and ceased, a unity temporarily associated with plurality, a micro-deity within distorting man's true perspective, in Buddhist doctrine of all illusions the most dangerous.

In poetical diction, on the other hand, the poet not infrequently apostrophizes his past subjective experience as a serial unity or continuum, *chitta* being in this case the term evidently current for such a device, to the exclusion of *mano* and *viññāṇa*. Similarly our own poets select 'heart' or 'soul' for their monologues, never 'mind' or other terms; witness Goethe:

"Herz, mein Herz! was soll das geben?...
Ich erkenne dich nicht mehr!"

"O heart gone gadding after things that please...
I call thee, heart, the breaker of my luck!
I call thee, heart, despoiler of my lot!"[34]

I will restmin thee, heart, as elephant
Is by the towngate's sallyport..."[35]

"'Tis thou, O heart, dost make us what we are..."[36]

This choice of *chitta* as the sensuous and impulsive consciousrness contrasted with the more intellectual aspect of it, make the word 'heart' in such passages a fitting counterpart for *chitta*—heart, that is, in the popular diction of to-day. Three centuries ago only, as we know, the word could bear a more intellectual significance, seen in such Biblical phrases as: "Out of the heart proceed evil thoughts. . ." and: "Why reason ye in your hearts?" 'Heart' (*hadaya*) also finds a place in Buddhist popular psychology, but in the sense of 'inmost,' 'inwardness,' and also of 'thorough.'[37]

In this aspect of sensuous and impulsive ungoverned mentality, *chitta* is likened repeatedly to an ape, tricksy, restless and inconstant, inquisitive and greedy:

"Within the little five-doored hut an ape
Doth prow, and round and round from door to door
He hies, rattling with blows again, again...
Halt, ape! run thou not forth! for thee
'Tis not herein as it was wont to be.
Reason doth hold thee captive. Never more
Shalt roam far hence [in freedom as of yore]."[38]

Dhammapāla, in his Commentary on the poem, refers to the *chitta*-ape of the Nikāya simile,[39] albeit the emphasis there is on the transient coming and passing of mental pulsations:

"Just as an ape in the forest, roaming through the woodland, clutches a bough, lets go and clutches another, so is what is called

chitta, *that is, mind. . . ever changing as it arises and ceases."*

"Unsteady is the heart as jigging ape!"[4]

is another instance of a figure that became the type-symbol of *chitta* or *viññāṇa* in Buddhist pictorial art.[41] So is the Sutta-Nipāta line:[42]

"They grasp, they clutch, then loose their hold again,
As monkey gripping bough, then letting go,"

where *chitta* is involved in concrete action; as it is again in the *Saṃyutta* version of what we know as the negro's Brer Rabbit and the Tar-Baby:

"In the Himālaya, king of the mountains, are pleasant glades where both monkeys and men may roam. There trappers lay pitch-snares in the monkey-tracks. . . . And if a monkey is foolish and greedy, he takes up the pitch in his paw and it sticks there. Seeking to free his paw with the other, it sticks to that. Seeking to free his paws with one foot. . . with the other foot, it sticks to both. Seeking to free both feet with his snout, it sticks to that."[43]

The moral points to self-control and governance of sense-impressions and sense-desires. Elsewhere we find mind not as truant, but as guide and governor, under the Platonic simile of charioteer:

"The body is a chariot light, mind is the charioteer, . . .

[where *mano* is the selected word, *chitta* playing a subordinate part, more in the sense of heart, as the loose, unattached drapings]

With steeds of equal training, mind pursues the mastered road. . . Smiting with wisdom's whip the team that makes for things of sense. Herein, O king, thyself alone must be the charioteer."[44]

(2) The belief in the ductability of mind by proper and persistent training, or 'taming.' as it was termed, was the other reason for the importance assigned to mental analysis in Buddhism. The proximate object of the higher or

religious life is described as *vinaya*, discipline, *sañyama*, restraint, *attānaṃ dameti, sameti*, taming, harmonizing one's self, and guarding the gates of sense.

"Once hard to tame, by taming nom is tamed Vīra . . . "

is one of many such emphatic verses.[45] The conquest by man's wit and minor physique over not only the horse, with his swiftness and natural weapons, but also over the mass and might and mind of the elephant, lifted the process of taming to a more impressive status. The latter beast, trained and otherwise, plays a frequent part in ethical similes, and the great Teacher is often termed

"Tamer and driver of the hearts of men."[46]

Other peaceful conquests by man are brought into service:

"The conduit-makers lead the stream;
Fletchers coerce the arrow shaft;
The joiners mould the wooden plank;
The self: 'tis that the pious tame!"[47]

The doctrine of self-mastery, with a varying co-efficient of asceticism, is common to all religions and practical philosophies worthy of being so named. Buddhism, as an intellectual or philosophical religion, combats the unruly faculties more with the mental analysis of the 'Know thyself' gnomon, than with the averted gaze of a faith appealing chiefly to emotion and will. Its 'middle way' between self-indulgence and asceticism is, in one Sutta, explicitly declared to be, not such an aversion of attention, but a system calling for the habit of breaking up the web of conscious experience, of classifying its factors, valuing them and mastering the issues in conduct.[48]

References

1. Cp. my *Buddhism*, pp. 67 f.
2. See below, p. 36.

3. *Anicca* (pron. *a-nitcha*).
4. *Saṃyutta-Nikāya,* vol. ii. p. 94.
5. *Majjhima-N.* i. 256 ff. (P.T.S. ed.).
6. *Dīgha-N.* i. 213; *Aṅguttara-N.* i. 170 (pron. *ma-nō, vin-yāna*).
7. *Saṃyutta-N:* i. 122, iii. 124.
8. *Dīgha-N.* ii. 63 (*Dialogues of the Buddha,* ii. 60—'consciousness' had been a better rendering for *viññāṇa*).
9. *Saṃyutta-N.* iii. 69
10. *Saṃyutta-N.* ii. 13,91, 101.
11. *Śatapatha-Brāhmaṇa,* xi. 2, 3 (*SBE* xliv. pp. 27 f).
12. *Chāndogya-Upanishad,* vi. 3; 2,3; viii. 14, I.
13. *Bṛhadāraṇyaka-Upanishad,* i. 4, 7; 6, 3 iii. 2, 12.
14. *Vibhaṅga,* 136 ff.; *Dhamma-sangaṇi,* §1309.
15. *Majjhima-N.* i. 53 ; *Saṃyutta-N.* ii. 3 f.
16. *Compendium,* 94 f.
17. *Majjhima-N.* ii. 32.
18. *Atthasālinī,* 308; see *Buddhist Psychological Ethics,* 175, *n.* I.
19. *Op: cit.* (*SBE* xxxv.) i. 86.
20. *Saṃtyutta-N.* iii. 120; iv. 47 ; *Aṅguttara-N.* iii. 255; 267f.
21. *Aṅguttara-N.* i. 149.
22. *Saṃyutta-N.* i. 169.
23. *Aṅguttara-N.* i. 53.
24. *Ibid.,* iv. 114.
25. Ibid., iii. 65.
26. *Aṅguttara-N.* i. 57.
27. *Ibid.,* iii. 211.
28. *Saṃyutta-N.* i. 72.
29. *Dhammapada,* verses 379f.
30. *Majjhima-N.* i. 120, 242.
31. For more discussion, but again very limited in scope, see my *Buddhism,* 1912, chap. iii.
32. *Vinaya Texts,* i. pp. 100 f.; the last part of the argument occurs frequently in the second, third and fourth Nikāyas.
33. *Dīgha-N.* i. 263.
34. *Thereagāthā,* verses 213–14 (cp. *Psalms of the Brethren,* p. 155).
35. Ibid., verse 355.
36. Ibid., verse 1127; verses 1106–45 are a continuous monologue to the *chitta.*
37. *Bud. Psy. Ethics,* Ixxviii.; and § 1343; below, p. 71.
38. *Psalms of the Brethren,* verses 125 f. So Shakespeare: "More new-fangled than an ape, more giddy in my desires than a monkey" (*As You Like It*); or Nietzsche on Sterne: "His squirrel-soul sprang with insatiable unrest from branch to branch."
39. *Saṃyutta-N.* ii. 95.
40. *Psalms of the Brethren,* verse 1111.

41. Ibid., p. 112. *n.* 2.
42. Verse 791.
43. *Saṃyutta-N.* v. 148; a similar case of self-capture occurs in the Jātakas or Birth-stories of the Sutta Piṭaka, and in Brazilian folklore (cp. A. Lang, *The Brown Fairy Book,* pp. 336 f.)
44. *Jātaka,* vi, p. 252. The rendering 'the soul is the charioteer' is only justifiable if the verse was *brrowed* by Buddhism. The Commentary explains as above. Cp the figure of the Self in the chariot, intellect (*buddhi*) driving, with the reins (*mano*) the horses of sense along the roads (objects of sense), in *Kaṭha Upanishad,* i 3, 3f.
45. *Psalms of the Brethren,* verses 8ff.; also *Sisters,* xxxii.
46. *Psalms of the Sisters,* verses 216, 135; *Brethren,* verse 1111.
47. Ibid verse 19; *Dhammapada,* 80, 145.
48. *Majjhima-N.* iii. 298; my *Buddhism,* 67.

3

The Psychology of the Nikāyas—*continued*

II. Consciousness and the External World

Self-Governance, as one of the two reasons for mental analysis in Buddhist culture, brings us up against the nature of that culture's inquiry into sense, and mental activity on occasion of sense. If we may judge by the space and the careful treatment allotted to it, the importance of the subject finds no parallel in the history of human ideas until we come to modern Europe. We find, it is true, no philosophical basis for it comparable to our theories of Sensationalism, Experientalism, or Rationalism. But we can see man conceived as a compound of instruments receptive and reacting; conceived, too, as standing Janus-faced, with the power of looking into one of two houses—the house of sense-impressions, or mundane experience, and the house of spiritual impressions, including what may be called supernormal experience.[1] Between these two vistas he had to shape a course of conduct as sane, and attended by aspirations as worthy, as those instruments, moulded by past karma, were able to form.

Those 'instruments' may be enumerated Buddhist-wise thus:

> *"She taught to me the Norm, wherein I learnt*
> *The factors, organs, bases of this self—*
> *Impermanent compound."*[2]

What are these 'factors, organs, bases' according to 'the Norm,' or orthodox doctrine?

The Five Aggregates

'Factors' here stand for *khandhā* (Sansk *skandhāh*), literally heap, body, or aggregate. These are the *nāmarūpa*, dealt with in the last chapter, but the division is now fivefold: four immaterial or incorporeal (*ă-rūpiĭo*) aggregates or groups, and one material aggregate.

Under this category we see a fuller effort made to take account, not so much of a dual, as of a still more composite nature in the so-called individual. We see also the refusal to recognize therein any unity except that which is conferred, for practical convenience, by the bond and label of the name—person, individual, creature, self and the like. The five may be translated: material qualities, feeling, sense-perception, complexes of consciousness or co-efficients, and, fifthly, consciousness itself, the *viññāṇa* of foregoing remarks. There is here no *order* in function or evolution. Buddhaghosa, in one dissertation on them,[3] takes the last after the first, much as we should do, in order that the middle ones 'shall be better understood.' But in the Canon no reason for the order, which as stated is invariable, is ever given.

The division is as old as the inception of the Buddhist movement itself. It forms part (together with the doctrines of the ethical mean, or Middle Path, the Eightfold Path of supreme or 'right' practice, the Four Truths, and the vision and goal of saintship) of the first sermon or Sutta, ascribed to the Founder. And it is a cardinal doctrine of the Theravāda all the way. There is no evidence that any such fivefold category was current at the time, although each term was in use. That which is apparently peculiar to Buddhism is the grouping of them as a division exhaustive, not only of body and mind, but also of such terms as might serve to stand erroneously for the notion of a perduring hyper-phenomenal soul or self. Other classifications of the factors of individual being occur throughout the Canon,[4] some twofold, some three, some fourfold, but not one is systemically maintained as is that of the *khandha*'s.

The word itself occurs but once in an early Upanishad, meaning 'body' of doctrine (*dharmaskandha*),[5] and once again in a later Upanishad meaning 'mass' of smoke.[6] Nor does the word occur among the psychological terms of the Sānkhya aphorisms. This may point to a relatively deliberate choice of the word and of the division by the founders of Buddhism.

That a word so static in import should have been chosen in view of the dynamic tendency of the doctrine, and of the canonical exposition given of the khandhas, is somewhat curious. Buddhaghosa helps us out to some extent by pointing out that, whereas *khandha* signifies aggregate (*rāsi*), it also has a comprehensive and symbolic, lit. contracting, import. Thus, just as we say when a man hews at a portion of a tree, he is cutting 'the tree,' so do we mean when we use such a comprehensive term as, say, *viññāṇak-khandha.*[7] And perhaps no other term could so well have served to keep the plurality, the absence of essential unity in the individual, so forcibly to the fore as this clumsy-seeming word. The oldest interpretations of the five terms are, for that matter, of anything but static import. Let us consider these in the accepted order:

> *"Why, bhikkhus, do ye say* rūpa*? Because one is affected by* (modified by, feels, ruppati):*—affected by cold and heat, by hunger and thirst, by touch of gnat and mosquito, by wind, and sun and reptiles."*[8]

Rūpa, in its more special sense, is a *visible* shape, a coloured surface, the object of vision. More generally, it means those material qualities, both of, and external to, the individual, through movements and changes in which he becomes aware, receives impressions of sense. '*Ruppati,*' which I have rendered 'affected by,' is, in Buddhaghosa's comment on this passage, paraphrased by disturbed (or excited), struck (or impressed), hurt, broken (or disintegrated),[9] the verbal form being deponent. We have no term that quite fits. 'Matter' suggests stuff, materials, irrespective of sentience-producing quality. 'Body' suggests framework, solidity, object of touch. 'Form,' often used for *rūpa,* is of much philosophical ambiguity, for so far from suggesting the mutability of *rūpa,* it stands, in Aristotelianism, for the "constant element as contrasted with the shifting shapes of matter."[10] Hence no one term will suffice for constant duty. For *rūpa,* as an 'aggregate' or factor of a living organism, material, or corporeal aggregate, or simply 'body' may prove near enough. And in any case, the text and commentary clearly attach no *substantial* significance to the literal meaning of *khandha.* 'Aggregate' refers only to a manifold, an accumulation, an indefinitely repeated class of phenomena, implied when any part of them is discussed. Instead of any static thing or things, there is here defined a type of process, an incessantly changing and modifiable flux, expressed in terms of sentience, or of what modern text-books might treat of under metasomatism or metabolism.

With regard, next, to the second *khandha*:

"Why, bhikkhus, do ye say, vedanā? *Because* vedanā *are felt* (vediyanti). *And what are felt? Both pleasant and painful and also neutral* vedanā. *Each is felt, therefore ye say feelings."*

Vedanā has often been translated by sensation, partly perhaps because the stem, from √*vid,* suggests the senses as sources of *knowledge,* partly owing to the position of *vedanā* in the series of terms constituting the formula of causation: "because of the sixfold sphere of sense, contact; because of contact, *vedanā*; because of *vedaniā,* craving . . " But the hedonistic content of the term requires the word 'feeling,' a term with which, for that matter, our worried psychologists know that a deal of sense-import is mixed up. By Buddhists the third and the fifth aggregates are more closely associated with sensations than is *vedanā.* 'Contact,' 'touch,' produces both sensations and *vedanā*:

"Just as, bhikkhus, from the juxtaposition and friction of two

sticks, warmth is generated, heat is born; and from the altering, the relinquishing of just those sticks, that corresponding warmth is allayed and ceases, even so does pleasant vedanā *arise because of contact capable of producing it . . . and cease when the contact ceases.*"[11]

(The same applies to painful *vedanā.*)

But 'contact,' as a philosophical term, has the very general implication of proximate condition, either physical, or, in the case of *vedanā,* psychical.[12]

Now feeling in this, its strictly hedonistic sense, cannot be expressed in more intimate terms. It means more essentially state of the subject, or subjective state, for our psychology, than any other phase of consciousness. The Buddhists discerned this too, not only in the reply describing *vedanā,* but also in the warning added in Buddhaghosa's comment, namely, that "there is no distinct entity or subject who feels;" "it is only feeling that feels or enjoys," and that "because of some object which is in causal relation to pleasant or other feeling."[13] So consistently insistent is Buddhist philosophy in giving prominence to object over subject—to see in *object* the relating thing, and in the compound, labelled 'subject,' the thing related.[14] "In philosophy," says our neo-Realism, "the mind must eliminate itself."[15]

A point of interest to psychologists is the recognition of neutral feeling, with its doubly negative name:—not-painful-not-pleasant (*adukkha-m-asukha*) feeling—as a distinct phase. A positive content indicated by a negative term need appear no anomaly to us, for whom 'immortality,' 'independence' are accepted instances. Our psychology only doubts whether bare feeling can be said to arise in subjective experience, unless it be felt as pleasant or unpleasant. Between these two we are disposed to allow no more than a zero-point.

In one Sutta, a layman maintains the European preference for two phases only of feeling as the more authoritative doctrine.[16] The Founder is referred to and replies, that feeling may be classed under two, three or more heads according to the special aspect of feeling discussed by the teacher. For bare emotional sentience, the three phases are invariably given. The typical description of them, in the archaic analysis of the Nikāyas, runs as follows. The teacher is the eminent woman-teacher, Dhammadinnā, whose answers on this occasion are confirmed by the Buddha as being what he himself would have said. After stating the three phases, and qualifying each as being either bodily or mental, she is then asked:[1]

" '*What has pleasant feeling that is pleasant, what that is painful? What has painful feeling that is painful, what that is pleasant? What has neutral feeling that is pleasant, what that is unpleasant?' 'Pleasant feeling has stationariness as pleasant, change as unpleasant, painful feeling has stationariness as painful, change as pleasant. Neutral feeling has knowledge as pleasant, not-knowing as painful.*' "[18]

After replying to an ethical question, she is asked:

" '*What is comparable to pleasant, to painful, to neutral feeling?' 'Pleasant and painful feelings are mutually comparable. Neutral feeling is comparable with ignorance, as this is with knowledge.*' "

It is not easy for us, with our logic of definition and division, based on Greek Substantialism, to acquit Buddhists here of confusing 'bare feeling,' 'feeling proper,' with intellectual concomitants. Personally, however, the longer I study their thought, the more reluctant I become to vote them illogical, even from our own logical standpoints. I am inclined instead to judge that they envisaged pleasurable feeling less comprehensively than we do, and that they may have seen in what Bain, for instance, called emotions of relativity, emotions with a preponderant intellectual coefficient, an irreducible base of simple or bare feeling not describable as 'pleasant.' Such feeling we might describe negatively as neutral, positively as intellectual excitement: the residual consciousness in the complex state called *pīti*, interest or zest.[19]

Fuller acquaintance with Buddhaghosa may reveal more

light hereon. For all purposes of religious and moral edification, this third phase was of little use, as compared with the other two. In the Suttas it is chiefly of concrete consciousness predominantly 'happy' and 'unhappy' that we read. But the cultivation of neutral feeling was of considerable importance in the exercises for the attainment of that other-world consciousness, alluded to in the first chapter.

In this second aggregate too we can see that there is no question of static substance or state quickened or otherwise modified in, or by feeling, but only a plurality of moods. The 'heap' simply records the fact of a quantity of past experiences of similar emotional gushes.

We come to the third *khandha*:

"Why do ye say saññā? Because one perceives (sañjānati). *And what does one perceive? One perceives blue-or-green,*[20] *and yellow and red and white."*

This scant information with respect to such an everyday word doubtless sufficed for the hearers, but its simplicity is misleading for alien readers. *Saññā* is not limited to sense-perception, but includes perceiving of all kinds. Our own term 'perception' is similarly elastic. In editing the second book of the Abhidhamma-Piṭaka,[21] I found a classification distinguishing between *saññā* as cognitive assimilation on occasion of sense, and *saññā* as cognitive assimilation of ideas by way of naming. The former is called perception of resistance, or opposition (*patigha-saññā*). This, writes Buddhaghosa,[22] is perception on occasion of sight, hearing, etc., when consciousness is aware of the impact of impressions; of external things as different, we might say. The latter is called perception of the equivalent word, or name (*adhivachănă-saññā*), and is exercised by the *sensus communis* (*mano*), when *e.g.* "one is seated . . . and asks another who is thoughtful: 'What are you thinking of?' one perceives through his speech." Thus there are two stages in *saññā*-consciousness: (1) "contemplating sense-impressions;" (2)

"ability to know what they are" by naming. An illustration is added, in the Commentary, of a bhikkhu contemplating a woman who sat spinning as he passed, and on his companion taxing him therewith, said it was because of her likeness to his sister.

We may conclude, then, that in this third or perception-aggregate, we have the content of any consciousness, or *chitta,* in so far as there is awareness with recognition, this being expressed by naming.

As to the fourth aggregate:

"Why, bhikkhus, do ye say sankhāra's*? Because they compose what is compound* (sankhătaṃ). *And what is the compound that they compose? They compose material quality* (rūpaṃ) *as compound to make* (lit. in order to[23]) 'rūpa;' *they compose feeling as compound to make 'feeling;' percepts, to make 'percept;' complexes to make 'complexes;' consciousness to make 'consciousness.'"*

"Just as one cooks rice-gruel to make rice-gruel," continues the Commentator, "or a cake to make a cake, so is this being brought together by antecedent conditions and wrought up into a [mental] compound termed *rūpa* . . . . By 'composing' is meant 'striving along, kneading together, effecting.' Together with the mental production of *rūpa* are compounded the feeling and other states associated with it. The essential mark of a *sankhāra* is 'being work of mind.'"[24]

The fourth *khandha,* then, is the complementary factor to the more passive, receptive phase of consciousness. In the somewhat later elaborations of doctrine in the Abhidhamrna-Piṭaka, this constructive aspect is reserved for the first-named of the 52 elements of consciousness comprised under *sankhāra*'s, namely, *chetănā.*[3] In that term Buddhists discern what we mean by volition. The other 51 factors are rather coefficients in any conscious state, than pre-eminently active or constructive functionings. To this manifold of factors we shall have occasion to return.

Lastly:

"Why, bhikkhus, do ye say viññāṇa? it is conscious (vijānāti),

therefore it is called viññāṇa, *consciousness. Of what is it conscious? Of tastes: sour, bitter, acrid, sweet, alkaline, non-alkaline, saline, non-saline."*

Here it will be said: if this and the third, or perception-*khandha*, are merely awareness of difference in sensations, what is there to choose between them? If we turn to one of the psycho-ethical discussions of the *Majjhima-Nikāya* to help us out, we shall find apparently the same conclusion arrived at. The questioner is Koṭṭhĭta, called the Great, and Sāriputta, chief of the disciples, and although no class of students attending either is mentioned, the dialogue must have been compiled, or actually delivered for the benefit of brethren less proficient than the eminent Mahā-Koṭṭhĭta.[26] The questions turn on the nature of *viññāṇa* and other aggregates. The first is here said to be consciousness of what is pleasant, painful, and neither. A little later, feeling is declared to be concerned with the same, and perception, with sensations such as colour. Koṭṭhĭta then goes on :

" *'And that, brother, which is feeling, that which is perception, and that which is* viññāṇa, *are these mental states conjoined, or disconnected ? Are you able to disentangle them and point out different modes of action for them?' 'The three, brother, are conjoined, not disconnected, nor are we able to disentangle them and point out for them different modes of action. For what one feels, brother, one perceives; what one perceives, of that one is conscious.'"*

The essential homogeneousness of *chitta* or *chitta*'s would seem to be here upheld, as a corrective against attaching too much weight to analytic distinctions. *Viññāṇa,* we are assured on good Buddhist authority, is of more general import than anyone phase of consciousness. It there includes and involves the other three mental aggregates just as our own psychologies allow only a logical distinction for purposes of analysis between two or more main phases of consciousness. To see further separateness would be, wrote Buddhgahosa;[27] "as if one drew water at the delta where the five rivers enter the sea saying: 'This is Ganges water; this is Jumna water.' All these mental states are one with respect to their object." "Sensations of sight," he adds, "illustrate perception here, because form and appearance show its action most clearly; sensations of taste are cited for consciousness as best showing its awareness of specific distinction [in general]."

Viññāṇa, in fact, being, it would seem, a term of such general import, may stand for any 'awareness' of mind, no matter how general or how abstract the content.

It must still remain for us a logical anomaly to see the more general aspect *co-ordinated* with the more special aspects, as one among four aggregates, instead of the second, third and fourth being reduced to subdivisions of the fifth. Some day we shall witness a Thera of Ceylon or Burma, master of both his own and our traditions, doing justice to the subject. Meanwhile we may do well to hang up our judgment on two memoranda: (1) the absence in the Buddhist tradition of any cogent logic of division by way of genus and species; (2) the presence of an emphatic negation of any substantial unity in *viññāṇa* or *chitta* or *mano.* Safety was felt to lie only in classifying mind as not one, subdivided, but as several. *Nāmarūpa* was far more convenient as a starting-point, but it was a dangerous old bottle for new wine, for it dated, as we have seen, from animistic or ātmanistic compilations. "Why," wrote Buddhaghosa, "did the Exalted One say there were five aggregates, no less and no more? Because these not only sunl up all classes of conditioned things, but they afford no foothold for soul and the animistic, moreover they include all other classifications."[28] No 'wrong view' finds, in the Nikāyas, correction so emphatic, so uncompromising as this: that "*viññāṇa* is an identical something, continuous, persisting."[29]

Hence the primary reason for the khandha-division was practical—the reader may call it religious, philosophical, ethical, as he pleases—and not scientific. Herein it resembled Plato's threefold pysche—sentient, passionate, rational—put forward to inculcate the governance of the first and second by the third. Aristotle's threefold scheme was more scientific, giving us "an evolutionary concept of increasing connotation."[30] But Aristotle was elaborating a tradition which started from unity, and held it 'most unreasonable' to consider the psyche as a plurality.[31] The founders of Buddhism, ascribing to that unity in 'self,' to which consciousness usually, and language (when not metaphorical) always testifies, only the validity of popular, conventional usage, started from plurality. They saw in the person a plurality held together by a name, and by an economy of mental procedure. Their philosophy is synthetic, starting from many. When it analyses, it reveals, not fractions, but a number of co-ordinated ultimates. For it, ultimate truth lies in inverting conventional truth, or as we might say, common sense. The latter sees truth in a consistent use of names for things-as-perceived, holding that these are things-as-they-really-are (*yathābhūtaṃ*). But the task of philosophy lay in 'penetrating' through these fictions of the 'world's' beliefs and these myths of language. It must not take surface-usage as in the least trustworthy. The attitude is of course common to all philosophizing worthy of the name. But in Buddhism it was *applied* in a more thoroughgoing degree than almost anywhere else in ancient thought. By 'him who sees,' the 'one,' to which consciousness seemed to testify, is considered as a myth carried over from the name, and valid only in popular thought.

Theory of Sense

The next word in our verse is 'organs': *āyătănă.* This word, meaning simply place or sphere for meeting, or of origin, or ground of happening,[32] is used to cover *both* organ of sense and sense-object. The 'meeting' is that effected, on occasion of sensation, between organ and object. What this meeting of man's cognitive apparatus with the external world consisted in, was, as we know, variously conceived. But no serious effort to inquire into, and formulate, the natural procedure in that meeting appears in any Indian literature judged to be pre-Buddhistic, or contemporary with the Nikāyas.[33] Vedāntic inquiries in this direction are late, probably incited by Buddhist pioneering effort.

Nothing, however, were further from truth than to affirm that the late Vedism, or the early Vedāntism of the oldest Upanishads took no account of sense in their philosophy. When our historians of psychology have realized that to limit their origins to Hellenistic thought is to present inexcusably mutilated work, we shall find our facts more accessible. The crabbed confines of a little manual prevent due justice being dealt to the many interesting glimpses of sense-theories in the eight Upanishads generally reckoned oldest.[34] But a few words on them are necessary to show both how much and how little the advance in theory by Buddhism had to aid it.

Summarized, these glimpses show much psychological insight, fitfully and unsystematically presented, often with a poetic Platonism. All are more or less subservient to the main ātmanistic theory.

(1) How little that theory, as compared with Buddhist pluralism, was calculated to encourage serious independent inquiry, appears in such phrases as: "Let no man try to find out what sights, sounds, smells, tastes are. Let him know the seer. . . the hearer," etc. Again: "When seeing, He (Brahman) is called 'eye,'" and so forth; "He is eye of the eye, ear of the ear," etc. He, or It, used these instruments, but was distinct in essence, separable. When they slept, he unsleeping went whither he listed, 'golden person, bird-alone.'[35] Accordingly the listeners did not 'try' very much. Nevertheless, they saw vividly some things of significance for psychology.

(2) With a view concentrated more on theoretic synthesis than on the facts of experience, they now included, now excluded, the three relatively animal senses of smell, taste and touch. Sometimes only one is excluded; *e.g.* the indwelling Ātman or Brahman 'pulls,' or 'rules' eye, ear, tongue (not tasting, but speaking), and skin, but not the nose.[36] So, too, these four only are called 'graspers,' and the

respective objects, 'overgraspers,' for "eye is seized by visible objects, ear by sound," etc.—a notion equally applicable to the senses of smell and taste.

(3) One result of this aesthetic eclecticism is that the significance of touch in our knowledge of the external world is not discerned. Thus it is of the eye, and not of touch, that we read: "The essence (sap) of the material, the mortal, the static [Deussen: *Stehendes, sthitan*], the actual [Deussen: *Seiende, sat*] is the eye, for it is the essence of *sat* (being)."[37] In one Upanishad action and hands replace touch and sensitive surfaces.[38]

(4) But the tenderency to centralization in the person went along with a theory of the co-ordination of sensations into the unity of percepts, by the action of a *sensus communis* or sense-mind (*prajñā*). Thus: "Some say, that the vital forces (*prāṇa's*) go into one becoming, since no one could at the same time make known a name, see . . . hear . . . think with *manas* . . . whereas the vital forces, by going into one becoming, bring all these one after another into consciousness, . . . and then all function together with each one, sight, hearing," etc.[39] And it is in the heart that these vital forces, which include the senses[40] become one. The heart is thus the *sensorium commune.*

(5) We do not find the Buddhist common name for the peripheral organs of sense, as door or gate, but only 'openings' (*suṣayah*) into the heart, *viz.* eye and ear, speech, mind and air.[41]

(6) In the heart too reside all *rūpa*'s, "for we know colours by the heart," while the sun, or the sun-god, abides in the eye.[42] Here we seem to get a fleeting glimpse—no more—of a parallel to the Common and Special Sensibles of Aristotle's theory of sense, developed in modern psychology by Locke as primary and secondary qualities. Deussen translates *rūpa*'s by forms, but the context, let alone the Buddhist *tradition*, requires us to see in the object of sight strictly colours, as Max Müller renders it.

We shall now be the better able to judge wherein Buddhist

psychology may be considered to have made any advance on these striking, and often mythically, or at least figuratively, conceived theories of the nature of sense. Confining ourselves, as in the foregoing chapter, to the earliest documents, and taking counsel on them from the Commentaries, we will take the six matters numbered above in order.

(1) We have already seen, we know, that to what extent the obsession of the Subject, omnipresent yet indwelling, may, have checked inquiry into contact with Object, Buddhism had shaken off the cause of such a check. So thoroughgoing was the doctrine, in refusing to emphasize, or even recognize, any self-agency that might be misconceived, when the law of causation was being discussed, that queries in terms of a personal agent were deemed unfitting.

"There are four foods, bhikkhus, for maintaining creatures that have come to be, or for conducing to their coming to be. What are the four? Material food, gross or subtle, secondly, contact; thirdly, mental provision; fourthly, viññāṇa. These are the four."

The Commentator explains that in cases 2 and 3 the interlocutor might easily understand something ancillary to the food itself, as when (2) birds feed their young, causing contact, and as when (3) a turtle lays her eggs not in the water but on the sand above its reach. But the new *viññāṇa* that becomes potential in the new embryo as the *result* of a last conditioning, *viññāṇa* in a dying person, was not so easy to bring under the notion of food—food for a complete new *nāmarūpa.*

"Thereupon the venerable Mōḷiya Phagguna said to the Exalted One: 'Who is it, lord, that feeds on the food viññāṇa?*' 'Tis no fit question,' said the Exalted One. 'I do not use the term "feeds." If I did, your question were a fit one. But since I do not, if one were to ask: "For what is* viññāṇa *a food?" this were a fit question; and this the fit reply:* Viññāṇa*-food is the condition for bringing about rebirth in the future.*[43] *When that is come to birth there is the sphere of sense and of the condition of sensations, namely, contact."*

"'But who is it, lord, that comes into contact?'

"''Tis no fit question,' said the Exalted One. 'I do not say: he comes into contact. . . . If one were to ask: "Because of what condition is there contdct?" this were a fit question, and this the fit reply: Conditioned by the sphere of sense [arises] contact; conditioned by contact [arises] feeling."

"'But who is it, lord, that feels?'

"''Tis no fit question . . . '"[44] [and so on, for yet two more unfit queries : who desires? who grasps?]

(2) Whether the concentration of Object, and not on Subject, was the cause or not, Buddhist analyses consistently deal with the five senses, and with each of them. The priority invariably yielded to Sight and Hearing may be a legacy from older doctrines. But whatever is stated about the nature and functions of sanse, is shown as valid for each of the senses. So faithfully is this uncompromising consistency carried out, that the application of statements of each sense, taken severally, is effected at a considerable cost of literary effect and of readers' patinece.[45]

The most general (as well as the earliest) formula of sense-consness, given half a dozen times in the *Majjhima* and *Saṃyutta Nikāyas,* is as follows:

"Because of sight [lit. eye] *and visible matter* (rūpa) *arises visual consciousness* (chakkhu-viññāṇa) *the collision of the three is contact. (Conditioned by contact* [*arises*] *feeling; what one feels, one perceives; what one perceives, one thinks about; what one thinks about, one is obsessed withal; hence obsessions concerning past, future and present objects cognized through sight beset and infest a man.) Because of hearing. . . of smell, etc."*[46]

The formula ceases at the first bracket. The context is given to illustrate the application. Here is another application, taken from the 207 short Suttas on the sphere of sense:[47]

"Viññāṇa *comes to pass, bhikkkus, because of a dual [thing]. What is that dual [thing]? Because of sight and because of visible object arises visual consciousness. Sight is transient, changing, its state is becoming-other-ness.' Visible, objects are just the same. So this dual thing is both mobile and passing away . . . . Visual consciousness, sprung from a condition, from a relation which is transient, changing, having 'becoming-other-ness,' is itself no less so. Now this kind of consciousness, happening because of a transient condition, whence shall it become perduring? Visual contact—as the collision, coincidence, encounter of these three phenomena is called—is transient, changing, having 'becoming-other-ness.' Arisen because of a transient condition, whence shall it become perduring? Come into contact one feels, is aware, perceives; hence these states also are mobile and passing away, transient, changing, having 'becoming-other-ness.'"*

This protracted formula is repeated for each sense.

As to the psycho-physical nature of this contact, no attempt is made throughout the canonical books to analyse it. Nearly or quite a decade of centuries was needed for so academical, so scientifically disinterested an advance as this. But we can imagine that, for a country, whose archaic analyses could locate colours (or visible objects more concretely conceived) 'in the heart,' the seat of mind, it was no difficult matter so to transcend the bare *touch*-notion in contact as to feel no need for either a material medium, or for the outleaping *eidôla*-emanations of old Greek thought.[48]

Whatever was actually held to take place in all contact, we find no underlying hypothesis of an *illusory* world, or of a *creating* intelligence within. The association of *māyā*, the cosnlic 'illusion' of other and later Indian thought, is absent from the whole of Theravāda Buddhism. Its ultimate data were phenomenal, and yet they were very real. They were not dependent upon a constructing percipient mind. The manifestation of sensations in experience depended, in part, on the external elements being brought into suitable focus with organs made of similar elements, within us. Without, there was the ever-mobile, ever-changing world compounded of countless syntheses of the four elements: the extended, the cohering, the calorific, the mobile, with or without the residual element of life. Within, were mobile and changing syntheses of all these elements. To effect contact of sense between the without and the within, a threefold conjuncture was needed. After discoursing on the four elements as external and internal, each of them taken separately, Sāriputta, the leading teacher after the Buddha, is represented as saying:

"*If* (1) *the action of the eye is not cut off, but* (2) *external visible objects do not come into focus,*[49] *and* (3) *a correlation according is not set up, there is not to that extent the lnanifestation of a corresponding degree of viññāṇa.* [The same results from conditions 1 and 2 only being given.] *But if the action of the eye is not cut off, if external visible objects come into focus, and if a correlation according is set up, then the corresponding degree of consciousness is manifested.*"

This is repeated, as is usual, for the other senses in turn. The widespread theory of 'like being known only by like' was considered to be implicit in these, the mother-doctrines. The elements were either (*a*) belonging to the self or internal, or (*b*) external.[50] Later it is referred to as an ancient doctrine.[51] But speculation concerning nature or mind is not a Buddhist characteristic. We find the more positive statements that variety in contact is due to difference in organ or in object. And from difference in contact, difference arises in feeling, perception, volition, etc.[52]

The picturesque metaphor of 'grasper' and 'over-grasper' for sense-organ and object I do not find in the Nikāyas. There are other metaphors,[53] most of which are for ethical, or for what we might call evangelical exhortation. But in two or three there are points of philosophical interest. In the Sutta called 'The Snake,' of the Sense-sphere Saṃyutta,[54] a man ('Everyman') is represented as fleeing for his life from four great snakes (the four elements), five assassins (the five aggregates or *khandhas*), with Love-of-pleasure in their midst with drawn sword. He hastens into a village, which he finds empty and about to be destroyed by bandits. Rushing away he comes to the perils of the sea, to cross which he has to make a raft, and scull him self over with hands and feet. Here the empty village is identified with the six organs of sense, wherein no 'headman,' no 'I,' nor 'Mine' is found.[55] In this connexion it is well to remember that the very ancient superstitions concerning 'the man that is seen in the eye' became, in the older Upanishads, a symbol of the indwelling agent, whether conceived as divine or human: "*that* is the Ātman . . . the immortal . . . Brahman."[56] Again the village-sacking bandits are the six kinds of 'external' objects of sense, for each organ of sense is hit (*haññati,* smitten, hurt, slain) by objects that are attractive or the reverse.

(3) It was only natural that the uncompromising, unflinching way in which Buddhism, from the outset, faced the *whole* question of sense-cognition, and its moral effect on man should eventually lead to interesting developments, such as the nature of touch and things tangible (*phoṭṭhabba*), and the relation of touch to sight. But this is developed in post-Nikāyan literature (pp. 143, 186).

(4) The theory of a co-ordinating factor in sense, or *sensus communis,* is adopted in both early and scholastic Buddhism. The five special senses had mutually distinct provinces:

> *"These five senses, brother, have different fields, different ranges; they do not share each other's field and range. Of them thus mutually independent,* mano *is their resort, and* mano *partakes of, enjoys, the field and range of them all."*[57]

Buddhaghosa's comments on this theory of mind as an organ of reference are mainly figurative, but of interest. As to the word rendered by resort (*paṭisarăṇa*), this he illustrates elsewhere on this wise:—Disciples sometimes invite the Master's teaching by saying: "Things (or phenomena) have the Exalted One as their root, their guide, their resort. Well for us if he reveal the meaning of this that he has just declared . . . ."[58] Hereon the Commentary's parable: "Things of all four planes [of being], coming into the focus of his omniscience, are said to resort to the Exalted One, they make him their resort, they go down, they go down together. . . . Thus contact comes to his discernment asking: 'What is my name?' 'Thou art contact in the sense of searching.' . . ." The four mental aggregates ask in turn, "'each receiving a name according to its nature.'"

In commenting on the *Majjhima* passage, where 'mind' is the 'resort,' he first distinguishes between the work of *mano* as 'five-door cognition' (*i.e.* on occasion of sensations) and as 'mind-door' (or representative) cognition. Then he proceeds: "Visual consciousness is mere seeing visible object; and so for the other senses. There is here no scope for the three radical states of appetite, ill-will and bewilderment. These affect cognition proper (*mano,* or *jăvănā*)." He then illustrates by a king enjoying a large revenue accumulating from numberless little taxes levied from a village of five families. Finally, in commenting on the dry, non-ethical formulas of the Abhidhamma-Piṭaka concernjng *mano,*[59] he states that whereas the door-objects—sight, sound, etc., impressions—are variables that pass by, *mano,* having its 'base' in the heart, is a constant which has the sole function of receiving them. "The mark of *mana* is the cognizing, the becoming aware of sense-objects immediately after the visual, or other sense-consciousness." Thus, through *mano,* we get a simulated unity and simultaneity of impressions, which are really single and successive, if exceedingly and most delicately swift.

This location of intellectual functioning in the heart as its basis or 'site' (*vatthu*) has been carried over by Buddhaghosa and his contemporaries from pre-Buddhistic tradition. Nevertheless the psycho-physical association is not made in the canonical books. And modern Buddhists, jealous for the omniscience of their great Founder, maintain that this silence is not accidental; in other words, the Buddha judged that to assign another, *e.g.* a cerebral, basis for mind would not 'go down' with his age. Be that as it may, the evasion of the word, 'heart' is quite marked. After enumerating the bases of the five senses, the Paṭṭhāna goes on: "That material thing on the basis of which apprehension and comprehension take place. . . .,"[60] 'Heart,' in the Canon, comes into purely poetical idiom, as among ourselves to-day, *e.g.* 'peace of heart,' 'tribulation of heart,'[61] 'appealing to the heart,'[62] and 'heart of the Norm,'[63] or doctrine.

(5) Similarly, the expression doors (*dvāra*), or gates of sense, which became a technical term in the scholastic psychology of cognition, is in the older books but a picturesque simile. The only *formula* in which it there occurs is in that of sense-control called 'guardedness as to the doors of sense.' But that the figure was ready, even in the earlier days, to fall into rank as a scientific term, and may even then have been often so used, appears from a parable in the Nikāyas of a 'six-gated fortified city' through the gates where of come messengers, bringing a true message. The moral is that there are more ways than one of apprehending the gospel. And the six gates are explained to be the six organs of sense, 'mindfulness' being the doorkeeper.[64]

(6) The properties of things, whether primary or secondary or otherwise, were much discussed in mediaeval Buddhist philosophy. The English reader can discern this in the numerous quotations given by S.Z. Aung in his notes to the *Compendium.* But the Nikāyas had an ethical philosophy, theoretical and practical, to put forward. And no inquiry was wrought up into the Suttas save such as was judged necessary or auxiliary to the attainment of 'right views' in such a philosophy, and to the application of them to practice.

The honesty and candour of the Suttas, in dealing with the fact of knowledge as got by way of five peripheral 'doors' and one inward 'door' of sense, and with conduct as impressed and incited and swayed by sense, are due to a conviction of the immense importance of understanding this fact of life, and all that the fact involved for the mind and conduct. Cognition through sense was a process of natural causation. Through sense arose feeling; through feeling, action. Hence the importance of treating the subject without eclecticism, without restheticism, from the standpoint of natural law, for a practical purpose. This was, in ultimate terms, the elimination of the ills that arose through sense-cognition, and through the actions to which mankind was thereby impelled.

Reference

1. *Majjhima-N.* i. 279.
2. *Psalms of the Sisters,* verses 69,43 ; *Brethren,* 1255.
3. *Visuddhi-magga,* ch. xiv.
4. Cp. my *Buddhism,* p. 72
5. *Chāndogya-U.* II. ii. 3.
6. *Maitrāyaṇa-U.* 7, 11.
7. *Atthasālinī,* 141.
8. *Saṃyutta-N.* iii, 86 (*Kandha-Saṃyutta,* 79).
9. *Sāratthappakāsinī.*
10. *Compendium,* S.Z. Aung on 'Rūpa' pp. 271 f.
11. *Majjhima-N.* iii, 242.
12. *Atthasālinī,* 109.
13. *Sāratthappakāsinī.*
14. *Compendium,* p. 2.
15. S. Alexander, *Things and Knowledge.*
16. *Saṃyutta-N.* iv. 223f.
17. *Majjhima-N.* i. 303.
18. Or as Buddhaghosa's less awkward prose paraphrases: "in netural feeling a state of knowing is pleasant, a state of not knowing is painful."
19. See below pp. 94, 97, 176, 187.
20. *Nīla;* the word does duty for both, for the colour of sky, cloud, hills, trees, etc., *Bud. Psy. Ethics,* p. 62, *n.* 1; cp. Edridge Green, *Colour-Blindness and Colour-Percepption:* "The *terra-chromic* regard blue as a greenish violet." India is the home of blue- green indigo.
21. *Vibhanga,* 1904, p. 6.
22. *Smmoha-vinodanī,* Commentary on the *Vibhanga.* An English edition is in preparation.
23. The Siṃhalese printed edition of the Commentary reads *rūpatthāya,* and so for the other terms.
24. *Chetayita,* literally, 'being *mind*-ed.'
25. In its more passive sense of component things, rather than compounding function, *sankhāra* has a much wider implication, even that of 'things in general,' 'this transient world,' and the like. I may refer readers to S.Z. Aung's analysis of the rterm in our *Compendium of Philosophy,* pp. 273f., and to R.O. Franke's Appendix in his selected

translations from the Dīgha-Nikāya (1913). I much regret that the *Compendium* was not in Dr. Franke's hands when he wrote this Appendix. It could have had no juster or more appreciative critic. His own rendering of this difficult term is *'Hervorbringungen,'* products.'

26. *Majjhima-N.* i. 292 f.
27. Commentary on *Majjhima-N.* Sutta 43.
28. *Visuddhi-Nagga,* ch. xiv; cp. Warren's *Buddhism in Translations,* p. 156.
29. *Majjhima-N.* i 256; quite literally, 'runs on, flows on, not-other.'
30. G. Croom Robertson, *Elements of Philosophy,* p. 221.
31. *De Anima,* ch. iv.
32. Threefold meaning assigned by Buddhaghosa, *Commentary on Dīgha-Nikāya,* 2, 124.
33. It is perhps significant that the words *Sinn* (sense) and *Empfindung* (sensation) do not even occur in Deussen's index to his work on the Upanishads or to those of vols. i. and ii. of his *History of* (Indian) *Philosophy.*
34. According to Regnaud these are *Bṛhadāraṇyaka, Chāndogya, Kaushītaki, Aitareyya, Taittirīya, Īśā, Kena, Kaṭha.*
35. *Bṛh.* iv. 3, 12.
36. *Bṛh,* iii 7, 17f.
37. Ibid, ii, 3, 4.
38. The *Kaushītaki.*
39. *Kaush,* iii. 2.
40. *Chānd,* iii. 12, 3 f and *n.* 1; viii 3, 3.
41. Ibid., iii, 13, 11 f. The word 'door,' *dvāra,* is very near, however; see *ibid.,* iii. 13.6.
42. *Bṛh,* iii. 9, 20.
43. *Saṃyutta-N.* ii. 13.
44. An indimatic phrase of popular usage: 'things seen heard, imagined, apprehended,' or 'things seen, heard, touched, imagined,' occurs, but not where sense-cognition is dicussed. It survives in part; see *Compendium,* p. 37.
45. *Majjhima-N.* i. iii f.
46. *Saṃyutta-N.* iv. 67. f.
47. Even Aristotle only makes some sort of medium for sight after condition (*De Anima,* II. vii.).
48. Literally : avenue. *Majjhima-N.* i. 190.
49. *Majjhima-N.* i. 421 f.
50. *Atthasālinī,* 313; *Bud. Psy. Eth.* lx.
51. *Saṃyutta-N.* ii. 140f.
52. *Bud. Psy. Ethics,* p. 175, *n.*4.
53. iv. 172 f.
54. *Atthasālinī,* 309 ; and *Sārătthăppakāsinī* on this Sutta.
55. *Chānd.* iv. 15, I; viii. 7, 4; *Bṛh.* iii. 7, 18.
56. *Majjhima-N.* i. 295; *Saṃyutta-N.* v. 218.

57. *Aṅguttara-N.* i. 199, and elsewhere. *Paṭi-sarăṇa* is literally 're-going.'
58. *Bud. Psy. Ethics,* lxxxviii, 129 *n.*1 *Attasālinī,* 263 f.
59. Pointed out by S.Z. Aung; *Compendium,* pp. 277 f.
60. *Saṃyutta-N.* i. 126, 212; *Anguttara-N.* v. 46.
61. *Dīgha-N.* iii. 173.
62. *Vbhaṅga,* 401.
63. *Saṃyutta-N.* iv. 194.

4

The Psychology of the Nikāyas—*continued*

III. Feeling

The last-named feature is the reason why, in the lengthy collection of Suttas devoted to the 'Sixfold Sphere of Sense,'[1] we get so open and steady a contemplation of the psychology of sense, and so limited a range of psychological result. We are told that the six senses give man his world, his everything—that they *are* the world, everything.

"I will teach you Sabbaṃ [the all, everything] . . . . *What is that? Eye and visible object, ear and sound, nose,"* and so on to *mano* and its 'objects.'[2]

"I will teach you the arising and the passing away of the world. . . . What are they? Because of eye and visible form arises visual consciousness, the encounter of the three is contact. . ., thence feeling, thence craving, from the extinction of which comes extinction of grasping and the extinction oj this whole mass of ill."[3]

"That by which one becomes cognizant of the world, and has conceits about the world, that is called, in the Ariyan discipline, the world. . . namely, by cognizance through sight, hearing, smell, taste, touch, mano."[4]

"I say, that the end of the world is not to be learnt, to be seen, to be got to, by going to the end of the world, nor by not getting there is an end to be made of ill.[5] *. . .'Tis even in this fathom-long carcase, percipient, intelligent, that I declare to be the genesis of the world, the ceasing of the world and the way going to the cessation of the world."*[6]

We should err if we read any Idealism into the last quotation; it is anticipated by a context coinciding mainly with the foregoing quotation, which is again closely connected with those before it. The elements of ultimate reality, I do not say existed, but were constantly becoming and passing away, in the macrocosm as in the subjective microcosm. But that microcosm apprehended them by way of its sense-doors. They presented the 'world' to the individual by representing it.

"Where there is eye and visible objects, visual consciousness and the things that may be learnt through visual consciousness, there is the world, or the notion of world. Where there is ear," etc.[7]

Those sense-doors were presenting it to him night and day from birth till death, and, by the all-powerful lever of feeling, were pushing him this way and that, as mighty Gaṅgā was ever bearing down bubbles of foam and driftwood.[8] And nothing that sense-cognition could show was able to end Sorrow and Pain finally and altogether.

So we hear more often about *how* sense affected than about *what* it told.[9] I have attributed this emphasis to the resthetic vivacity of the ancient Northern Hindus, as betrayed by their literature.[10] There is also this *negative condition*, under which Buddhist doctrine was put forward and organized: the absence of any advance in natural science.

Modern psychology has made its most marked forward strides during periods of scientific advance and excitement. And tpe strides were usually made by men of scientific, especially medical, training. Hartley, *e.g.*, was a physician; Tetens, a physicist and mathematician; Priestley was a chemist; Cabanis was a professor of medicine; Locke was a student of natural science and a physician; Weber, Fechner, Spencer are other notable instances. Such thinkers were more interested in the mechanism of sense as so many avenues of knowledge, and as a department of the science of the living organism. Their interest was intellectual. The 'dynamics' of consciousness were relatively uninteresting until the influence of Schopenhauer had leavened thought.

To revert to older days, it is clear from Aristotle's works that a considerable activity in biological inquiry was being carried on at the time, and that not only by Aristotle himself, 'master of those that know.' He too evinces a relatively mild interest in the dynamics of feeling and will. He delivered lectures on Ethics, but it is not a little instructive to compare his somewhat paedagogic treatment of Pleasure with the immense ground-wave importance attached to pain and pleasure, sorrow and happiness, in Buddhist psychological ethics. He writes six and a half sections, out of a total of ten, in the Nicomachean Ethics, *before* resuming thus: "The consideration of pleasure and pain. . . is one of the subjects we are bound to discuss, for we said that moral virtue and vice have to do with pleasures and pains, and most people say that happiness implies pleasure." In the *De Anima* and the *De Sensu*, his chief interest is in biological and intellectual conclusions.

But in the Buddhist canonical books, amid all the allusions to contemporary activities, there is no indication of any activity in scientific research going on, with the exception of astrology and medicine,[11] and of medicine rather practised as an art than as being advanced by systematic investigation and experiment.

The art of the physician and the surgeon figures frequently both in narrative, in sanitary regulation (*e.g.* in the Vinaya books), and in parable. The Founder himself is called the Great Healer, the World's Physician.[12] The most central of all Buddhist ethical doctrines—the Four Ariyan Truths—is formulated on the plan of a medical diagnosis: namely, the *nature* of a malady, its *cause*, its *cessation*, its *curative régime.* And we may not be greatly wrong if we judge that, however we regard the grasp of universal causation by the mind of the Sākyamuni,[13] it was due to (1) the absence of a contemporary body of science, and (2) the presence of a developed medical tradition, that the doctrine of causation took the, to us, peculiar form and standpoint that it did.

Thus: anything due to an assignable cause was terminable it you could stop the working of the cause. But you could stop it, because nothing became a cause arbitrarily, or supernaturally. Now, for the doctor, and for the patient and the patient's own folk, the 'anything,' the One Thing, is *Dukkha,* Ill (the word means everything that is the contrary of *Sukha*—happiness, pleasure). And all or any *dukkha* can be made to cease, if (1) it be rightly diagnosed, (2) its cause or the conditions of its genesis and persistence be ascertained, (3) the nature of the state contrary to it be realized, (4) the 'cure' consistently carried out.

The medical inspiration, or at least, standpoint, was pointed out several years ago by Dr. Kern:[14] "It is not difficult to see that these four Satyas are nothing else but the four cardinal articles of Indian medical science, applied to the spiritual healing of mankind, exactly as in the Yoga doctrine. *E.g.* in *Yogasūtra* ii. 15, Commentary: 'Just as the doctor's code is fourfold: illness, cause of illness, health, medicine, so too is this code fourfold, to wit: *saṃsāra,*[15] its cause, emancipation (*mōksha*), the way thereto.'" The learned writer, however, in this valuable *aperçu,* specializes unnecessarily, and moreover leaves us to draw a mistaken inference. I have heard a physician pointing out the analogy between the Four Truths and his own British medical code, from simply hearing them stated as Buddhist rpligious doctrine, without allusion being made to his own profession. Talking of physicians tempts me to quote from the letter of a notable British Buddhist as bearing on this point: "The operation and hospital-experience was indeed a very formidable affair—so terribly impressive in its insistence on the Dukkha-Truths, that I marvel . . . after that experience, that the realization of the truth of them is not more common, at least among those who have to do with hospitals. Perhaps indeed this most impressive object-lesson *is* responsible for the large proportion of medical men among those Occidentals who are . . . deeply interested in Buddhism."

Moreover, to quote the *late* Commentary on the *Yoga-sūtras* as an authority for the statement that Indian medical procedure had suggested a fundamental doctrine of Buddhism, is much as if one were to say that J.S. Mill's inclusion of the syllogism in his Formal Logic proves it to have been in existence when Aristotle was teaching. There were 'cardinal articles' of medical clinic, not only in India, but in all countries before either the *Yoga-sūtras* (let alone the Commentary) or other records, more certainly pre-Buddhistic, were compiled.

Here, however, I am concerned only to suggest that an advance in the systematic study of mind is especially liable to be influenced by, and to mould itself upon, that body of more or less systematic physical knowledge, which bulks most impressively in the more thoughtful part of the society of that time and place. For the subject-matter of mental science is, as we know, not accessible to strictly collective observation; introspection is of the individual, and in the individual no two instances of a phenomenon can be shown as absolutely coincident. Henee it is largely, I do not say only, when some onward stride in physical science draws the rest of human knowledge in its wake, that the laws of mind are freshly investigated, as something that must also be brought into the line of march.

Where there is no such advance in psychical investigation, some system of dogmatic metaphysic is probably holding the cultured imagination of the age captive, through the spell of some myth of the Word. When the mind breaks free and looks deeper, there will naturally be a recourse, for its fresh concepts, to more positive ideas as guides and supports.

Now in the healing lore and craft of the day—the only one, I repeat, that comes *prominently* to the front in episode and in details of rules in the Vinaya—the revolt of thought embodied in the Buddhist movement found its noblest inspiration. The word *dukkha* covers all that is meant by 'not well'—ills and pains of body, ills and misery of mind, in a word, dis-ease. Its presence is the doctor's *casus belli* and *raison d'être*; its cause and extinction is his quest. For its absence there may be several positive expressions. And yet there is nothing else in life so mortally positive as *dukkha*. And it is easy, alas! for many to conceive its mere absence as sufficient for happiness. Nibbāna itself, a quasi-negative term, was at times employed as = health,[16] as well as happiness. And the Founder, in one of his more emphatic utterances about his mission, expressed that as one of healing:

*"Both then and now just this do I reveal:—*dukkha *and the extinction of* dukkha."[17]

The physical healer finds the causes of dis-ease in the mutual interaction of man and his environment. Buddhism too found therein the causes of all that made for unhappiness. Sense-impressions were the avenues whereby came satisfactions (*pasādā*) fraught with peril. Consciousness, with its three main roots or conditions—greed or appetite, enmity, delusion—pushing it, reacted on its impressions as feeling, desire for, grasping after, all that tended to the expansion and conceit of this Me and Mine. And as it behoved the physician to keep in view all possible sources of any disease, neglecting none, so was Buddhism searching and exhaustive in its treatment of the avenues of sense, ignoring none of the five that conveyed, nor the sixth that co-ordinated and revived what the former brought.

The great intermediary between the (relatively) passive reactions to the manifold stimulus of sense and the following more or less deliberate reactions, Buddhism discerned, correctly enough, in Feeling. This might be pleasant, painful, or neither. And it did not follow that where feeling was pleasant (*sukha*), the symptoms of disease (*dukkha*) were absent. For the *sukha* born of sense was the most efficient handmaiden of *dukkha*, if *dukkha* be broadly understood as both physical and moral ill, and all that this does, or may involve of mental suffering and moral deterioration.

As Ledi Sadaw, the eminent Thera (Senior in the Order) writes:[18] "We must distinguish between *dukkha* of the category (or, in Buddhist idiom, of the essential mark) of some thing unpleasant experienced (by way of sense), physical or psychical, and the *dukkha* we use in the triad: impermanence (*aniccha*), ill, and non-soul (*an-atta*). By this *dukkha* we mean a state of peril and danger, without peace, security or blessing."

This, in other words, is the distinction a physician, or at least a patient, might draw between sensations of pain and disease. The presence, the growth, the decline of the pain is not always accompanied by the presence or increase or cessation of the disease. And this distinction we have to draw throughout the whole of Buddhist literature dealing with sense, with feeling, and the effects of feeling. Else we find ourselves landed in much inconsistency of expression, as I shall show.

That feeling is the inevitable response to awareness of new stimulus is affirmed up and down the Nikāyas, notably in *Saṃyutta-N.* on the sphere of sense (vol. iv. 1 fi.), *e.g.*:

> *"Where there are hands, there taking and setting down appears,. where there are feet, there coming and going appears,. where there are limbs, there folding and stretching appears; where there is stomach, there hunger and thirst appears. Just so, bhikkhus, where there is sight (or eye), or hearing . . . there arise subjective pleasure and pain, conditioned by sense-stimulus (lit. contact,* samphassa*)."*[19]

The contrary is then stated, both of the analogies and the analogues: ". . . Where there is not sight, etc., neither pleasure nor pain, conditioned by sense-stimulus, arises."

This quotation is conclusive enough to represent all other passages stating the concomitance of sensations and feeling, understood as our psychology of sense understands pleasure and pain, or at least pleasure and unpleasure.[20] That the senses convey pleasure as well as its opposite, is not only allowed and affirmed by doctrinal teaching, but the pleasure is also recognized as very genuine and good by the most eminent of the teachers. The Founder affirmed at times that none lived more at ease (*sukhaṃ seti*) than himself, however much he had forsworn most of the so-called good things of life.[21] His chief apostles forgather with him one fine evening in the Gosinga Wood, delighting in the 'divine perfumes' of the dewy moonlit scene, where the tall sāl-trees stand clad in golden bloom.[22] Temperance was prescribed for maintaining the physical comfort (*phāsuvihāra*) of health.[23]

But when the disciple is bidden to look upon *sukha* as, or *quâ dukkha*, then we know that the wider concept is to be understood after the *quâ*. And this is no less the case when things unpleasant to the 'average sensual man' are valued by a different scale and held to constitute higher pleasure:

"Things seen and heard, tastes, odours, what we touch,
Perceive, all, everything desirable,
Pleasant and sweet, while one can say 'It is,'
These are deemed Sukha by both gods and men,
And where these cease to be, they hold it woe.

"What other men call Sukha, *that the saints*
Call Dukkha; *what the rest so name,*
That do the Ariyans know as happiness,
Behold a norm that's hard to apprehend!
Hereby are baffled they that are not wise."[24]

If we would not be baffled, it is with this wider implication that we must read those passages wherein each sense is declared to be *dukkha*, and not productive of either this or its contrary. If, using Ledi Sadaw's definition, we read into such passages as *"seeing. . . is sorrow. . ."* the wider sense of *dukkha*, thus:

"The eye, brother, is a faculty of peril and danger, bringing, as such, no peace, security or blessing; it is to understand this that the Exalted One is lived . . . ."[25]

and so on for the other senses, why, then we may not be unwilling to admit even for laymen the truth in this 'monkish' statement.

References

1. *Saṃyutta-N* iv. 1 ff., 'Saḷāyatana.'
2. *Ibid.*, 15-27.
3. *Saṃyutta-N.* iv. 87; cp. 52.
4. *Ibid.*, 95.
5. *Ibid.*, 93.
6. *Ibid.*, i. 62; *Aṅguttara-N.* ii. 48.
7. *Saṃyutta-N.* iv. 39.
8. *Ibid.*, iii. 140. 179.
9. *Buddhism,* 'The Norm,' p. 65.
10. *Ency. Religion and Ethics,* 'Asceticism (Buddhist).'
11. Possibly also of mathematics; but there is no positive evidence.
12. Cp. *Psalms of the Brethren,* verses 722, 756, 830, 1111.
13. See this more fully treated in ch. iv. of my *Buddhism.*
13. *Indian Buddhism,* Strassburg, 1896, pp. 46 f. *Satya* = truth.
14. *Saṃsāra* = endless living and dying.
15. *Majjima-N.* i. 509; *Sutta-Nipāta,* verse 749.
16. *Majjhima-N.* i 140; *Saṃyutta-N.* iv. 384.
17. *Ymaka,* ii, Appendix, p. 248 (London, Pali Text Society, 1913).
18. *Saṃyutta-N.* iv. 171.
19. I owe this term, borowed from German science, to my univeresity colleague, Mr. T.H. Pear.
20. *Aṅguttara-N.* i. 136 f; *Saṃyutta-N.* iv. 127.
21. *Majjhima-N.* i. 212 f.; *Saṃyutta-N.* iv. 104 and *passim.*
22. *Bud. Psy. Ethics,* p. 353.
23. *Sutta-Nipāta,* verse 759f.; cp *Saṃyutta-N.* iv. 127.
24. *Ibid.*, iv. 51, 140.

5

The Psychology of the Nikāyas—*continued*

IV. Ideation

The *systematic* analysis of mind in the Nikāyas is pursued no further than the recipient and co-ordinating work of *mano* as *sensus communis.* Sequences in consciousness are occasionally pursued further, but without overmuch terminological consistency, and irregularly. Here are a few instances:

"Because of some tendency there arises perception, opinion, thinking, volition, wish, aspiration. And according as the tendency is low, mediocre or lofty, so will all these be."[1]

The process of conversion in religion is described as one of "hearing, attending, remembering, comparing, discerning, desire, zeal, pondering, endeavour."[2]

"Thinking results in desire, through desire objects are divided into what we like and what we dislike, hence envy and selfishness, hence quarrelling and fighting."[3]

"Conditioned by contact arises feeling; what one feels, one perceives,. what one perceives, one thinks about; what one thinks about, one is obsessed withal."[4]

These samples reveal the persistent effort, in the Suttas, to carry on the method, systematically observed in treating of sense, of setting forth mind and character as orderly, causal process. The method is emphatically Buddhist.[5] The most notable example of it is the important formula of natural causation, as exemplified in the process of life being bound up with *dukkha.* In the mental process, the resolution of afferent or receptive consciousness into efferent or discharging consciousness is clearly affirmed. Sense and feeling stirred by sense are converted into motor presentations; as desire, etc. But we meet with no closer analysis of intellectual process, of what has, in our own psychology, been called representative and re-representative cognition, or ideation. In the last sample, we only hear that 'what we perceive,' *i.e.* notice (the *saññā-khandha*), we 'think about' (*vitakketi*).

The latter term, with its substantive *vitakka* (from the root *tark*) is the most usual expression in the Suttas for the looser, popular meaning of thinking and thought: turning the mind on to a subject, mentation, adapting the attention. Without the prefix (*vi*), it is a term for argument or dialectic (*takka*).[6] It is used rather for restless and discursive intellection, and not for the *vol plané* of intuitive sweep of mind.

Another term, *vichāra,* used only in association with *vitakka,* is a complementary expression to this, indicating persistence in discursive thinking, the onset of which is indicated by *vitakka.*

A still more general term for intellection, without explicit reference to sense, is *chinteti, chintā,* but it is seldom met with in the older books.[7]

Another word, much used for the adapted attention, is *manasikāra,* literally mindmaking, work-in-mind.

Next, there are two words connoting representative cognition, in form much like our re-flect, re-consider—*pacchavekkhăti, paṭisañchikkhăti.* Both have the prefix of reversion and repetition, and both stems belong to the vocabulary of vision. The former, as with us, is also used for optical reflection. The Buddha thus admonishes his son Rāhula who is graduating in saintship:

"What is the use of a mirror?' 'To reflect, lord.' 'Even so must we reflect, and reflect in all our work of body, speech or thought, namely,

This that I would do, will it be harmful to myself, or others.' . . . "[8]

Closely allied to these terms are other two, less easy to render by exact equivalents: *săti* and *sampajañña*, mindfulness and discernment. The former term, with its compounds, *anussăti*,[9] used for reiterated recollection, and *paṭissăti*,[10] which throws emphasis on vivid reinstatement, are the Pali equivalents for 'memory' and its synonyms. But *săti*, an important term in Buddhist ethical training, is not wholly covered by memory, and is, on the whole, best rendered by mindfulness, inasmuch as it denotes rather the requisite condition for efficient remembrance, or thought of any kind, namely, lucidity and alertness of consciousness. It is a quality rather than a specific direction of consciousness; it expresses that heedful, 'thoughtful' awareness, which is the opposite of mental distractedness, and the essential preliminary to deliberate concentration of mind. But for all that, *săti* and memory are closely allied.[11] *Sampajañña* is more or less coincident with *săli*, and is usually employed in the Nikāyas as a twin word. It means literally 'sustained cognizing,' 'deliberateness,' 'self-awareness.'

"How is the bhikkhu mindful and self-aware? . . . He effects self-awareness in his going and his coming and all his avocations, in his speech and in his silence."[12]

The latter term is often rendered by 'self-possessed;' this expresses well the 'having one's self well in hand' of the Buddhist ideal. But our word is rather the condition, the requisite mental attitude in order to that moral victory. This is expressed in another of those mental causal sequences, from which I have quoted above:

". . . What is the nutriment (condition) of self-control? Sati-sampajañña.

"What is the nutriment (condition) of sati-sampajañña? *Thoroughgoing attention," etc. etc.*[13]

And 'self-possessed' does not make explicit the intellectual emphasis of *sampajāna*, as is done by Neumann's rendering of the twin phrase: *'klaren Sinnes und einsichtig,'* 'of lucid mind and discerning.' We might use 'self-conscious,' were this term and its substantive not somewhat debased in our moral and social currency. Moreover there is, in the Buddhist word, no explicit reference to 'self.' When in the Abhidhamma books of incipient scholasticism *sampajañña* came to be defined, it was ranked as a synonym among that galaxy of intellectual nomenclature, often repeated, in which consciousness, when engaged at its highest intellectual functioning, is described. But in so far as the word conveys an intellectual emphasis specifically its own, it is that of conscious or deliberate intellection. Thus *sampajāna-musā* is 'consciously speaking untruth.'[14]

In another brace of intellective terms, each of which is, in Abhidhamma, defined as equivalent to *sarnpajañña*:—*vichăyă*[15] and *vīmaṃsa*[16]—the emphasis is rather on the volitional coefficient, involved in discursive, inquiring effort of thought. *Chintā* also, and its verb, may take this more specific sense.'

*"There are four unthinkables, that may not be thought about [*i.c. *speculated about], involving for the thinker insanity and trouble. These are speculations concerning the range of Buddhaship, speculations concerning the range of him* [i.e. *of his intuitive powers*] *who is in meditative ecstasy, speculation concerning the working of* [*the law of*] *karma, and speculations about the world."*

The last kind of 'speculation' (*loka-chintā*) is by the Commentator defined to be on who made the world, or living beings, or the plant world, etc. The more usual word for speculation, conceived as a product rather than a process of thinking, is *diṭṭhi,* from *dṛś,* to see, and more allied etymologically therefore to our 'speculation.'

Coming to terms for cognition merging into preponderating volition, we have *chetănā, saiñehtanā* and *sankappa.* The first two, while connected etymologically with *chintā, chitta,* have come to mean purposive or volitional consciousness.

"I say that chetanā *is action; thinking, one acts by deed, word, or thought."*[17]

"Its meaning," wrote Buddhaghosa, "is co-ordinating; its essential property is effort, endeavour." And it is put in apposition with terms of wishing and aspiration.[18]

Sankappa (like *vitakka* above) emphasizes the mind being set on to some object. Mind as a planning, devising, designing, concocting, is a favourite notion in Buddhist psychology, as we saw under the fourth aggregate generally. It is the co-operative bustle of a bee-hive, in harmony with the pluralistic attitude.

Where there is a coefficient of pleasurable feeling, the intellectual interest, zest or excitement constitutes a state of mind termed *pīti*, about which more later. As an expansive, enthusiastic, but ethically desirable state, it is the complement to the self-restraint and calm held no less desirable.

Finally, there are all the names for the deeper or wider work of mind, when not busied with the details of ordinary reactions to sense. *Nāṇa* and *paññā*,[19] as knowledge or understanding, may face both ways, concerned either with sense or with higher things, but usually the latter. The second term is often likened to illumination, irradiation. Work of higher intellection is expressed in terms meaning penetration, insight, intuition, rather than by concepts of discursive thought, such as judgment, or ratiocination; reason—the 'reason' of Scottish psychology—ranks above reason-*ing*. And in the words *jhāna*, contemplation, and *samādhi*, rapt concentration, are contained the expression of that self-training in selective, intensive work of mind in which the Indian sought, by changing the usual conditions and procedure in cognition, to induce consciousness of a higher or different power.

Here, however, the special end served by the analysis of sense is no longer present, and consequently there is no systematic classification. We may say the same for the complex states of emotion and desire or passion. In the latter field we find only two mutually opposed groups of three: the three radical instincts of *appetite* (with its developments: greed, lust, passion); *aversion* (with its developments: anger, hate, malevolence, etc.); and *delusion* or *dulness* (equivalent to ignorance, confused consciousness). Three opposite instincts are reckoned as equally radical to these, but as they determine the conduct of the minority only of mankind, we hear much less of them, and they are, significantly enough, given in a negative form—*a-lōbha, a-dōsa, a-mōha.*[20] In this second group, however, *adōsa* appears under its positive name as *mettā,* that is, friendship, fraternal affection or love (*caritas, agapē*). And with it are prescribed, for systematic meditation, the other altruistic emotions of pity, or sympathy with suffering, and *mudn̆tā,* or sympathy with happiness.[21]

I know of no other groups to rank beside the systematic and easily systematized scheme of sense-consciousness, dealt with in a previous chapter. The reader will, I trust, not chafe at meeting these Buddhist concepts in their original dress. It seemed the least ambiguous way of showing what they really sought to convey.

In the succeeding centuries, however, when for a time the mental culture of India became largely Buddhist, the analysis and classification of states and processes of consciousness became extended and more explicit, as we shall see. In the venerable records under consideration, we must glean and infer here and there, to ascertain wherein the more complex, evolved, or 'higher' work of consciousness was held to consist. The following characteristics of mental activity, so reckoned, may carry us some way towards a correct synthesis.

1. *The complexity of any given* chitta *and its resolution*—This is markedly recognized in the opening book[22] of that somewhat later collection in the Canon known as the Abhidhamma-Piṭaka, in which the Nikāyas are frequently quoted as authoritative sources. But there is an interesting anticipation of the analytic procedure, followed in the first half of that work, in the *Majjhima-Nikāya.*[2] The Sutta is termed *Anupādā-*

Sutta or Series-Discourse, and contains an appreciation of the gifts and character of Sāriputta by the Master. Among these, his power of introspective analysis is referred to as "insight into the sequence of mental presentations;" and it is thus illustrated :

"For instance, bhikkhus, Sāriputta, aloof from sensuous desires, aloof from bad ideas, enters into and abides in First Jhāna, wherein attention is applied and sustained, which is born of solitude and filled with zest and pleasurable feeling. And the presentations in that First Jhāna, to wit, thinking applied and sustained (vitakka, vichāra), *and zest and pleasurable feeling* (pīti, sukha) *and singleness of object* (chitt'ekaggatā), *and contact, feeling, perception, volition, consciousness* (chitta), *desire* (chanda), *choice, effort, mindfulness, indifference, adaptation of attention* (manasikāra)—*these are for him serially determined; these, as they arise, are for him things understood, and as they are present and as they depart, are for him things understood. He discerns: 'Verily these presentations that were not, have become, having become, they again depart.' And he with regard to them abides neither drawn to, nor averse from them, independent, not captivated, but free, detached, his mind placing no barriers."*

This sound psychological attitude is attributed to the apostle equally in all other grades of Jhāna-exercises, the contents of consciousness varying, and discerned as varying, by one or more elements in the complex, from grade to grade. And the fact that in the exercise of this introspective intuition Sāriputta's fine intellect was distinguished, shows the extent to which Buddhist mental science recognized that work of intellection. Our manuals call it self-consciousness, internal perception, or the conscious relation of presentations to self-presentation: the realizing that 'this percept is mine,' *I* think this notion.' For the Buddhist this is the way in which the testimony of ignorant, untrained consciousness exercises introspection. But for the trained consciousness all introspection is retrospection—a fact recognized by our own psychology, though perhaps not by it sufficiently exploited to explain the apparent duality of subject and presentations. Thus each momentary present *chitta*, in introspection, is a complex of a present fact and past facts wrought up into it, both momentary. Hence Sāriputta 'retrospected,' but with no such reference to self. And that he had got beyond this illusive consciousness of a King Ego, holding a *levée* of presentations, was a source of great satisfaction to him.

"Now Ānanda saw Sāriputta coming afar off, and . . . he said to him: 'Serene and pure and radiant is your look, brother Sāriputta! In what mood has Sāriputta been to-day?' 'I have been alone, in Jhāna, *brother, and to me came never the thought:* I *am attaining it!* I *have got it!* I *have emerged from it !'*"[24]

For, in the Master's words:

"*. . . It is by holding up the idea of no-self with regard to all things without limit, that ye can say, 'I shall well discern cause and the arising of things through conditions.'*"[25]

To revert: any *chitta* or group of *chitta*'s— the *Dhamma-Sangaṇi* uses only the singular—was held to involve a number of factors, a complex content, divisible into the other three mental *khandha*'s or aggregates. And the trained intellect, if naturally acute, was able to divide and describe its immediately past complex as if it were a present, external collection of material objects. I say 'trained intellect,' not only with reference to the power of sustaining this analytic process in the detached, disinterested frame of mind praised in Sāriputta, not only to the absence of self-reference, but also to the fact that the process of internal perception implies a stock of classified concepts concerning states of consciousness, to which the introspector, in analysing, refers each phase or factor. Hence under this first feature in higher intellection must be reckoned: (1) an existing scheme of mental analysis reinstateable at will; and (2) the work of internal perception itself, consciousness referring consciousness not to a subject, but to partly or symbolically reinstated concepts, reinstated, that is, by way of the common name only: "this is desire, this is choice," etc. In a passage of the *Poṭṭhapāda Suttanta* we find internal perception distinguished by the name of *ñāṇa.* To Poṭṭhapāda's inquiry this reply is given:

"First arises the conscious state (saññā), *after that* ñāṇa (that is, insight concerning it). *The springing up of the latter is dependent on the springing up of the former. Thus he intuits: 'It is from this cause that* ñāṇa *has arisen in me.'* "[1]

2. *Intellect as a relating particulars to general concepts.*—This is what we have seen commended in Sāriputta. But I have now in mind certain large generalizations or abstract ideas, certain very general attributes which the trained mind, in Buddhism, had to discern in particulars. Prominent among these were the three universals: impermanence, ill, absence of self or soul (*a-niccha, dukkha, an-atta*). Under these, everything constituting the external world and the constituents of personal being were to be subsumed, or, in Buddhist idiom, everything was to be contemplated *quâ* these three: *anicchа-to,* etc. To be capable of this threefold insight as a habitual attitude of mind was the supreme intellectual criterion, the hall-mark of sound judgment.

To see all things as stamped with the 'mark' (*lakkhăṇa*): '*this* is transient,' etc., was not to be understood in the somewhat flabby and non-committing sense in which average folk will allow: '*Tout lasse, tout passe, tout casse,*' or 'man is born to sorrow,' and then 'pass by on the other side.' Nor was the third judgment—'nothing has any soul or substrate' (which is a development of the first)—to be made from a half-way stage. By this I mean, made from the platform of a knowledge which has merely outgrown the concepts both of primitive animism, and of mediaeval interpretations of Platonic realism and Aristotelian 'quiddity.' This threefold insight amounted to the three universal propositions: (1) that nothing in life and the world as known is really persistent save the fact of change; (2) that everything in life is, for the living sentient being, "a state of peril and danger, without lasting peace, security or blessing;" (3) that there is nothing in or of the living being exempt from the two foregoing judgments. That being so :

"Is it fitting to regard that which is impermanent, liable to suffering, having change as its nature, as . . . the self, the soul of me?"[27]

If it is imagined that this is affirmed of a perishable body and mind only, in other words, of the five aggregates, it should be noted that the early Buddhists found the current notions of *ātman*, soul or self, inextricably identifiable, or bound up with those constituents of the living being, which they at least covered by their *khandha*-category:

"*All recluses and brahmins*—all teachers, namely, of religion—*who consider the* ātman *as allocated in a variety of ways, consider that it is allocated in one or other of the five aggregates . . . namely, that* viññāṇa *is the soul, that the soul has* viññāṇa, *that* viññāṇa *is in the soul, that the soul is in* viññāṇa."[28]

and so for the other *khandhas*. But

"the learned Ariyan disciple, who discerns them that are Ariyans, and is trained and expert in Ariyan doctrine; . . . he understands that body and mind are impermanent, are liable to suffering, are without soul."[29]

Another such standpoint of the trained mind was

"clearly to see by right reason even as it really is this law of causation and these matters of life arising as [mutually] *conditioned."*[30]

(More of this in our next chapter.)

An interesting phase of this higher work of intellect is seen in the contemplative exercises called *Brahmavihāra*'s,[31] or as we might say, Sublime Occupations. A rather later term was "the four *Appamaññā*'s[32] or Infinites." This is where the intellect with a strong coefficient of emotion is turned from a particular to an ever-wider degree of generality. The coefficient emotions prescribed were, as stated above, love (*caritas*), pity, sympathetic joy, lastly indifference or equanimity, which was to replace this threefold succession, presumably as a bracing corrective to any excess of sentiment. The Nikāyan formula runs as follows:

"Come ye, bhikkhus, expelling the five Hindrances [sensuous desire, ill-will, stolidity-and-torpor, excitement-and-worry, perplexity, nescience] and attenuating the heart's defilements by insight, abide ye in the suffusing of one region of earth with a consciousness accompanied by love; thence the second region, thence the third, the fourth. And thus aloft, below, across, the entire world and all that are therein do ye continue to suffuse with a loving consciousness abounding, lofty, in finite, without anger or ill-will."[33]

This is repeated for each of the other three coefficients. The exercises, according to the testimony of the Nikāyas,[34] were not originally, or at least not exclusively, Buddhist. They were judged indispensable to the training of religious aspirants, and were known to pious laymen and held to be conducive to rebirth in the Brahma heaven. By earnest Buddhists they were practised as helps to that emancipation of heart and mind from all 'hindrances' and fetters adverse to spiritual perfection.[35]

3. *Intellect as a work of eliminating, prescinding, selecting.*— This inverse work of adjusted attention was considered no less important a branch of Buddhist mental culture. It is explicitly recognized in the Nikāyas, and was systematically practised in what was collectively known as *samādhi*, or concentrative meditation, or also as *adhichitta*, or higher consciousness.[36] Here again emancipation, the freedom of self-mastery, was the platform to be won, 'object, pith and goal,' as it was, of the higher life.[37] *Samādhi* is sometimes made to include the exercises just described.[38] And it is clear that to develop a concept in generality, in abstractness, the elimination of the concrete, of the particular, must proceed *pari passu*.

But the emphasis in *samādhi* is that of concentration, of an intensive attention, which can only be got by throwing overboard, into the sea of things disregarded and negligible, everything that is irrelevant and distracting to the single apex of thought (*chitt' ek-aggatā*), which is the equivalent term to *samādhi.*[39] Not only were objects of thought, presentations, percepts, etc., to be ejected, but the attitude, mood, movement of consciousness were to be regulated and modified deliberately. A dialogue between the Buddha and one of his leading disciples, Anuruddha, eminent for 'celestial vision,' a sort of 'second sight,' reveals this in some detail:

"Have you three, Anuruddha, leading this life, zealous, ardent and strenuous, experienced supernormal states, extraordinary Ariyan knowledge and insight, happiness?'

" 'We have perceived, lord, both an aura[40] *and a vision of forms. But lately these have all vanished and we do not attain to the after-image.'*

" 'But this is what you three must attain to. I too, indeed, before I became wholly enlightened and Buddha, perceived both aura and vision of forms. And then in my case too they vanished. So I pondered over the cause of this and discerned that concentration had left me, and hence the vision. Also that my concentration had been dispersed through access of doubt, then by want of attention, then by sloth and torpor, then by dread, then by elation, then by slackness, then by trying too much, then by sluggishness of effort, then by longing, then by awareness of differences. And to me continuing zealous, ardent and strenuous, came perception of aura and vision of forms. But they soon vanished again, because I contemplated the forms too closely. . . . Then I beheld the aura, but not the forms. . . then the forms, not the aura. . . then I beheld the one as immense, the others as small, and inversely. Finally, I judged that my shortcomings in concentration were varieties of vitiated consciousness, and that, these being all got rid of, I would practise threefold concentration, to wit, applying attention and sustaining it, sustaining attention without applying it afresh, and concentration without attention in either way. And I concentrated with rapture, and without it, with delight, and with

indifference. And then in me, with concentration so practised, lo! there arose the knowledge and the insight that my emancipation was sure, that this was my last life, that now there was no more rebecoming.'"[41]

The more usual process of systematic elimination of factors in consciousness was that known as the Four Jhānas. Jhāna (Sanskrit, *Dhyāna*), or ecstatic musing, was a practice of unknown antiquity, akin to what is generally termed *Yoga*. It is no-where. claimed in the Nikāyas as devised by, or peculiar to the founders of Buddhism. But no branch of mental culture appears oftener in the Suttas than this, or is more frequently prescribed for all serious study. I wrote several years ago,[42] that the psychology of Jhāna would one day come to evoke considerable interest. I believe that the 'day' is much nearer now, and further, that to what extent Jhāna is still practised in Buddhist monasticism, and to what extent proficients in it become accessible to inquiry, the medical psychology of to-day will find interesting material.[43] But I have nothing to add to the little outline there given of the process by which the Jhāna state was apparently brought about. That process was of the kind known, I believe, to hypnotism as auto-suggestion. There was no question of a subject placing a consciousness rendered as passive as possible at the disposal of another strongly volitional consciousness, as in what used to be called mesmerism. The *jhāyin* did not include a cataleptic condition in his programme save as an ultimate stage, not belonging to the so-called Four Jhānas, but to a four-or fivefold sequel of 'Arupa-Jhānas,' only attempted by experts, and as a final test or step to complete self-mastery and sanctification (—to call in a Christian term).[44] On the contrary, he was intensely conscious, but in prescribed, artificially induced ways. These, taken collectively, consisted in artificially intensifying that natural mental process, whereby the mind concentrates itself wholly, at the expense of general, many-sided alertness and awareness.[45]

There was first intense attention by way of 'an exclusive

sensation'—I believe it was Condillac who so defined attention. This was to be entered on after securing physical conditions as far as possible free from discomfort and disturbance, and with elimination of every kind of activity of body and of mind, save that of reacting to the bare sensation. After a time that reaction would practically cease, the wearied sense giving out. Change, indispensable to consciousness, has been eliminated, for the self-hypnotizer must not vary his source of sensations. Meanwhile the sensuous source, mark, or symbol is replaced by a representation of it, the percept by a corresponding image. So much is reckoned as preliminary or preparatory process. The image then becomes conceptualized or de-individualized and it is then, apparently, that a 'subjective sensation' of luminance or 'aura' is alleged to become felt,[46] and the subject experiences the supernormal consciousness of Jhāna proper, with or without its flashes of ecstasy.[47]

The Nikāyas nowhere describe the preliminary process in detail, and the very terms for the stages of it (such as *parikamma, upachāra,* etc.), belong to later books. But the list of material devices or *kasiṇa*'s—artifices I have called them—for inducing Jhāna by prolonged gazing, occur in these older books. They are stated as ten in number; those usually quoted being a portion of earth, a flame, or a colour.[48] The psychological interest of the process lies in the gradual elimination of certain factors of consciousness. The for-mulas run invariably thus:

*"When, aloof from sensuous ideas, aloof from evil ideas, he enters into and abides in First Jhāna, wherein attention is applied and sustained (*sa-vitakka, sa-vichāra*), which is born of solitude and filled with zest and pleasant emotion; when next, from the subsiding of attention applied and sustained, he enters into and abides in Second Jhāna, which is inward tranquillizing of the mind, self-contained and uplifted from the working of attention, is born of concentration, full of zest and pleasurable emotion; when next, through the quenching of zest, he abides with equal mind, mindful*

and discerning, experiencing in the body that pleasure whereof the Ariyans declare: 'Happy doth he abide with even, lucid mind, and so enters into and abides in Third Jhāna'; when next, by putting away both pleasant and painful emotion, by the dying out of the joy and misery he used to know, he enters into and abides in Fourth Jhāna, that utterly pure lucidity and indifference of mind, wherein is neither happiness nor unhappiness—this is the training of the higher consciousness."[49]

Here we have a gradual composure and collectedness of consciousness gradually brought about by the deliberate elimination of: (1) the restless, discursive work of intellect, seeking likenesses and differences, establishing relations, forming conclusions; (2) the expansive suffusion of zest, keen interest, creative joy; (3) all hedonistic consciousness.

The residual content of consciousness is, in the formula, admitted to be (*a*) a sort of sublimated or clarified *sati*, an intensified inward vision or intuition, such as a god or spirit might conceivably be capable of ; (*b*) indifference or equanimity, also godlike. This would be that neutral point of feeling, discussed in a former chapter, inclining from its equilibrium to pain at ignorance, and to pleasure at knowledge. And though pleasure is eliminated, the Jhāna-practice is spoken of collectively as belonging to happiness.[50] "Attainment in Jhāna," writes Mr. S.Z. Aung, "is a very important psychological moment, marking an epoch in his mental experience for the person who succeeds in commanding it. He has for the first time in his life tasted something unlike anything he has ever experienced before. The feeling is simply indescribable. He feels an entirely changed person, purged from the Hindrances. He is living a new, higher life, the life of a god of the heavens called Rūpa [or Vision],[51] experiencing the consciousness believed to be habitual there."[52]

I place on record these testimonies, ancient and modern, much as another might write of the alleged rapture enjoyed through the best European music, who himself was incapable of experiencing it. The contents of this sublimated Jhāna-consciousness, though severely pruned, do not appear to have been entirely, if at all, unearthly. It was usual for a disciple to ask his master for a theme, perhaps only a pregnant word or two, on which he might practise solitary meditation. And in the *Vibhaṅga*, the second book of Abhidhamma, the Jhāna- formula appears again and again with some such word inserted after each stage of Jhāna: *e.g.* love, or emptiness (*viz.* of soul); or again it might be one of the exercises in will, included in what came to be called the 37 factors of enlightenment.[53] Such a coefficient in the abnormal 'clearness of mind'[54]—a clarity to which mystics ancient and modern have testified—was not necessarily a matter for discursive or toiling intellection. Jhāna-consciousness, after the first stage, was beyond all that. It would continue to hold the notion in a species of penetrative contemplation, or intuitive beholding and comprehension. Thereafter, when normal consciousness recurred, it would be more strongly permeated than before with that notion, from the effect of this injection at high pressure.

A feature in the Jhāna-practice of the Nikāyas—I am not competent to assert as much either for modern Buddhism or Vedāntist Yoga—is the frequent and systematic recourse to it. It was for the brethren and sisters of the Order, what to all religious Christians, especially to those engaged in a religious calling, is the sacrament of the Eucharist—a function the psychology of which is curiously ignored in James's *Varieties.*[55] I have seen letters revealing some slight resemblance to Jhāna-consciousness at a first, or other communion. And there is a similar careful preparation of the 'heart' previous to communicating, as in the self-purging of the 'hindrances,' of the sensuous and immoral dispositions obligatory on a sincere disciple. No less, also, than communion was Jhāna practised, and with *mystic,* if not moral, success by those who were morally unworthy, though mystically predisposed. Jhāna was not end, but means, and not the only or indispensable means. But where the supernormal fits and flashes of other mystics are, by recorded testimony, fitful and rare, and not systematically led up to, Jhāna-consciousness would seem to have been habitually and voluntarily induced, if perhaps with varying degrees of success (*samāpatti*). There was of course this deep cleavage between it and the eucharistic consciousness, that the self was banished, and no sense of union with the divine One, or any One, aimed at or felt. Herein too the Buddhist differs from the Vedāntist, who sought to realize identity with *Ātman*, that is, the identity of the World-soul and his own self or *ātman—'Tat tvam asi'* (That art thou). Alone the *jhāyin* sat, but he did not 'flee alone to the Alone' exactly as did Plotinus.

And so far as such mystic sense of union implies passivity, Jhāna-consciousness is not on all-fours with most mysticism. To allude again to James's analysis; it has the essential *noëtic quality* too strongly to permit of passivity as a constant. Intellect and volition, for Buddhist thought, are hardly distinguishable,[56] and the *jhāyin* seems to be always master of himself and self-possessed, even in ecstasy, even to the deliberate falling into and emerging (as by a spiritual alarum-clock) from trance. There is a *synergy* about his Jhāna, combined with an absence of any reference whatever to a merging or melting into something greater, that for many may reveal defect, but which is certainly a most interesting and significant difference.

Of James's other two qualities of mystic consciousness—transiency and ineffability—the former is markedly true concerning the momentary ecstasy of attainment or *appaṇā* as also concerning the realization of great spiritual elevation generally. Touching the 'Fruit' of each 'Path' of spiritual progress appears to have been a momentary (*khaṇika*) flash of insight. As to the latter, ineffability, it is also true that we find no attempts by brethren who were expert at Jhāna, *e.g.* Anuruddha, Revata the Doubter, or Subhūti of the 'love-jhāna,'[57] to enter in detail into their abnormal experiences. The first-named Thera comes nearest:

"In fivefold concentrated ecstasy (samādhi)

My heart goes up in peace and unity.
Serene composure have I made my own;
My vision as a god's is clarified.
I know the destinies of other lives:
Whence beings come and whither they, do go;
Life here below, or other-where of life—
Steadfast and rapt, in fivefold Jhāna sunk."[58]

But although this celestial perspective is a staple article in saintly experience as recorded by the Nikāyas, and has a formula of its own, no seer ever gives it local habitation or actuality for mundane perception. Language is everywhere too much the creature and product of our fivefold world of sense, with a varying coefficient of motor consciousness, to be of much use in describing consciousness that has apparently got beyond the range of sense and local movement. Even in non-spatial perception of melody, we have to borrow from our sense of gravitational resistance. overcome, and to speak of rising and falling. Possibly, moreover, the symbols of communication, of description, become still harder to find for minds, whose articulate medium is not made rich and wieldy through familiarity with written words. Supernormal vision itself, on the other hand, might conceivably be stronger, freer, more accessible, in the absence of a bookish memory. But this point, though it may be relevant, I do not press. Many spheres of being, varying in remoteness, otherness, inaccessibility to his own earthly span of life, were very present to the Buddhist imagination. And denizens of the remoter, quasi-immaterial Brahma-spheres are represented as having to materialize in order to become perceptible to celestials less remote, let alone to human beings (*Dialogues,* ii. 244).

These remoter spheres were collectively called *A-rūpaloka,* or *Arūpāvachără,* world or sphere of the invisible or formless. Here there was life without instruments of sense or corporeality. And to attain, while yet on earth, to any conception (*per*ception was impossible) amounting to experience of a sphere, which was not spatial in a literal sense, there were four stages of *Arūpajhāna,* showing also an interesting, if very vague psychology. Elimination was now, not of factors of consciousness,—the clarity and the equanimity remain,—but of all consciousness of detail or of limitations, thus:

(1) "A bhikkhu, by passing beyond the consciousness of form, by putting an end to the sense of resistance, by paying no heed to the idea of distinctions, at the thought: 'Space is infinite!' attains to and abides in the conceptual sphere of space as infinite. For him his previous consciousness of things visible passes away, and there arises in him then the blissful consciousness, subtle yet actual, of an infinite sensation of space.

(2) "Again, a bhikkhu, having wholly transcended the sensation of infinite space, at the thought: 'Infinite is consciousness!' attains to and abides in the conceptual sphere of consciousness as infinite. For him the previous consciousness, subtle yet actual, of a conceptual sphere of space as infinite passes away. And he then becomes conscious only of a concept, subtle yet actual, of consciousness as infinite.

(3) "Again, having wholly transcended the conceptual sphere of consciousness as infinite, at the thought: 'There is nothing!' he attains to and abides in the conceptual sphere of nothingness. For him the previous consciousness, subtle yet actual, of a conceptual sphere of consciousness as infinite passes away. And he then becomes conscious only of a concept, subtle yet actual, of infinite nothingness.[59]

(4)". . . Having wholly transcended the sphere of nothingness, he attains to and abides in the sphere of neither-percipience-nor-non-percipience."[60]

After this either the subject emerged from Jhāna, or proceeded to fall into trance, perception and feeling ceasing.

On the fourth phase of quasi-unconsciousness, Buddhaghosa remarks: "[One might say] neither consciousness, nor etc. etc., as well as 'neither percipience, etc.,' so subtle and delicately faint is the consciousness."[61] We seem, in fact, to have come upon another limiting or zero-point, as was the case in 'neutral feeling.'

These curious and vague fetches of imagination may appeal in no way to modern readers, nevertheless they are serially, and in succession to the other four Jhānas, pronounced by the Buddha to be each a yet more exquisite happiness than its predecessor. This attribution is even made with regard to the final trance, the Teacher remarking, in reply to sceptics, that if no happiness could be affirmed of such a state, his statement was not made with respect to merely pleasant feeling, but with respect to any occasion whence happiness may be obtained.[62] Happiness is here evidently taken in the larger moral or spiritual sense, complementary to that wider sense in which, as we saw, *dukkha* might be used. If happiness was involved as a result of practising self-hypnotism and trance, happiness was, so far, associated with, and predicable of, that practice.

References

1. *Saṃyutta-N.* ii. 153; see Commentary.
2. *Majjhima-N.* i. *480;* ii. 173.
3. *Dīgha-N.* ii. 278 f. (*condensed).*
4. *Majjhima-N.* i., iii.
5. Not of course solely Buddhist. But it is interseting to compare, with the bose, cognate passages in the order Upanishads :—*Chāndogya,* vii. 226; *Taitirīya,* ii. 3–5; *Kaṭha,* i. 3, 10, etc.
6. *Dialogues,* i. 29, 34 f.
7. *Saṃyutta-N* v. 447; occurs not seldom in the *Jātaka* tales.
8. *Majjhima-N.* i. 415.
9. *Aṅguttara-N.* iii 284; v. 329; i. 30.
10. *Sutta-Nipāta,* verse 283; *Atthasālinī,* 147.
11. The reader of Pali may compare *sati,* in *Dīgha-N.* i. 180 and *Majjhima-N.* iii. 89. with *anussati, aṅussarati* in *Anguttara-N.* iii. 284 and v. 329.
12. *Dīgha-N.* i. 70.
13. *Aṅguttara-N.* v. 115.
14. *Majjhima-N.* i. 414; so *sampajāna-samāpatti,* deliberate abandonment of consciousness (in trance), *Dīgha-N.* i. 184.
15. *Ibid.* iii. 106; cp. *Atthasālinī* 147, with *Milianda,* 298.
16. *Dīgha-N.* ii. 222; *Vibhaṅga,* 222.
17. *Aṅguttara-N.* iii. 415.

18. *Saṃyutta-N.* ii. 99.
19. Pronounce *nyānya, panyā.*
20. Disinterestedness, amity, intelligence, *Aṅguttara-N.* i. 134f *Amoha* is synonymous with *paññā.*
21. *Ibid.*, 183.
22. Translated in my *Bud. Psy. Ethics.* Cp. below, ch. vii.
23. Vol. iii. p. 25. This was only published when my translation was practically finished; hence I have not referred to it there.
24. *Saṃyutta-N.* iii. 235 f.
25. *Aṅguttara-N.* iii 444.
26. *Dīgha-N.* i. 185.
27. *Saṃyutta-N.* iii. 104., and *passim.*
28. *Ibid.*, iii. 46, and *passim.*
29. *Saṃyutta-N.* iii. 57.
30. *Ibid.* ii. 26.
31. *Majjhima-N.* i. 369 f. See above, p. 95.
32. *Vibhanga,* 272 f.
33. *Saṃyutta-N.* v. 115f.
34. *Ibid.*
35. *Paṭisambhidā-magga,* vol. ii. pp. 130 f. *Mettā-kathā.*
36. *Aṅguttara-N.* i. 236 f.
37. *Majjhima-N.* i. 197; cp. *Aṅguttara-N.* ii. 26.
38. *Samyutta-N.* iv. 350 ff.
38. *Ibid.*, v. 21, 198, 225, 268; cp. *Dhamma-sangaṇi (Bud. Psy. Ethics),* §§ 11, 15.
39. *Obhāsa,* luminance.
40. *Majjhima-N.* iii. 157 f. I have considerably condensed the taxt. 'Practised' is literally 'made-to-become, developed. Cp. *Compendium,* 65f.
41. *Bud. Psy, Ethics,* lxxxviii.
42. I have unfortunately not seen a brochure on the subject by Surgeon-Major E. Rost (Rangoon).
43. *Majjhima-N.* iii. 28; *Aṅguttara-N.* iv. 456.
44. On the 'absence of mind' attained in Jhāna, see *Dialogues,* ii. 141. f.
45. Cp. *Yogāvacara's Manual,* ed. Rhus Davids, p. xi.
46. *Compendium,* 55.
47. *Aṅguttara-N.* i. 201; v. 46; *Majjhima-N.* ii 14; *Dīgha-N.* iii. 268.
48. *Aṅguttara-N.* i. 235, cf. 53; *Dīgha-N.* iii. 222, and *passim* in the Nikāyas. The last clause is peculiar to the first reference.
49. *Dīgha-N.* iii. 78; *Aṅguttara-N.* ii. 36, 87, *passim.*
50. It is conceived that in the heavens least remote from our sphere of being, sense is limited to vision and sound.
51. *Compendium,* p. 57.
52. *Ibid.*, 179 f; *Dialogues of the Buddha,* ii. 129.
53. Tennyson's testimony, supplied by Tyndall: "By God Almighty! There

is no delusion in the matter! It is no nebulous ecstasy, but a state of transcendent wonder, associated with absolute clearness of mind." Cp. the poem, 'Two Voices;' W. James's *Varieties of Religious Experience,* pp. 384ff.

54. See *op. cit.*
55. See above; *chitta, cheto, chintā, chetanā.*
56. *Psalms of the Brethren,* cclvi, iii. 1.
57. *Psalms of the Brethren,* verses 916f.
58. Here the mediaeval explanation is that the preceding stage of consiousness was discerned as, in reality, 'nothing'—an unsatisfactory exegesis, as it stands.
59. Cp. *Dialogues,* i. 249f. with ii. 118 f. *passim* in the Four Nikāyas. The second reference gives similar *samādhi* exercises.
60. *Sumaṅgala-Vilāsinī,* ii.
61. *Saṃyutta-N.* iv. 227 f.

6

The Psychology of the Nikāyas—*continued*

IV Ideation—*continued*

4. *Growth of intellect a vision of objects under the causal relation*—There is a wealth of terms in Pali and Sanskrit for knowledge under the aspects both of process and of product, for which it is hard to find a corresponding aboundance of, at least, English equivalents. We too have words from the metaphors of sight, access, grasp and piercing, and indeed have better exploited 'light.' But Buddhist philosophy has not only commandeered the acts of waking (*budh*) and turning-towards (*ā-vaj*, adverting), but has nearly a dozen words built on the proper 'know'-stems alone (*jan, vid*). And the question for the student of Buddhist psychology arises: how far does the greater richness of Buddhist intellectual nomenclature correspond to a greater manifold in modes of knowing or of knowledge?

There are even, in that psychology, terms for cognitive states which have a time co-efficient, implicative of either confident expectation or assured attainment. These are, respectively: 'consciousness-that-I-shall-know-the-unknown' (*anaññāta-ñ-ñassāmītindriya*) and 'consciousness of gnosis' (*aññindriya*).[1] (The affix '*indriya,*' here rendered by 'consciousness,' is literally power or faculty or ability, used in that general way in which we employ the word, 'sense,' but with a more dynamic import.) They are technical terms of spiritual experience. The former describes the mind of the convert, or, to revert to technical terms, of one who has reached the stream (*sōt-āpanna*). The latter term describes this mind as, 'going from strength to strength,' he attains each successive degree in the way to saintship. Final fruition involves a third technical term: *aññātāvindriya*, the consciousness of him who has gnosis, who has come to know.

More usually the consciousness of deepening power of intellection and, to speak in spatial terms, of a widening perspective, is expressed by the help of one of two adverbs: *yoniso* and *yathābhūtaṃ*. These have, both of them, the secondary meaning of 'thoroughly' and 'genuinely.' But in their literal sense they mean respectively 'from the source, or matrix,' and 'as [it has] become.' We approximate to this intensive force of import in the word 'radical,' and in the expression, made classical by Matthew Arnold, "seeing things as in themselves they really are." This cumbrous phrase cannot match the latter of the two Pali terms either in conciseness, or in *genetic* emphasis. But Arnold was not to blame for a weak spot in his native tongue, nor for the unfortunate conditions, whatever they were, which resulted in our dropping the strong term *weoröan*, and cheapening its weak substitute 'to become.' The makers and the heirs of modern French and modern German were more fortunate, or sounder in their thinking than we, when they preserved this most precious instrument of philosophic insight, the power of which was felt by Hegel, and is now being exploited by Prof. Bergson.

The full causative force of the two terms was doubtless lost, for Buddhists, by conventional usage. And yet I write the last phrase hesitatingly, for whereas they claim nothing novel in the use of them, it is not without significance that neither term is pre-Buddhistic in the sense lent them in the Nikāyas. Nor are they a feature in Vedāntist or in Jain literature.[2] As expressions qualifying a certain depth and direction of intellectual consciousness they are emphatically Buddhist. And since for Buddhism to know thoroughly was to know under the causal relation, was to know by way of judgments relating effect with cause,—the adoption of just these two qualifying phrases for such intellection as was deemed admirable, is full of interest.

Work-in-mind (*mănăsĭkāra*) which was not *yoniso* led to muddled results.[3] Coupled with 'the voice of another' it became the joint agent in arousing greed, hate and error.[4] But *yoniso-manasikāra* was essential to the prevention or suppression of the 'hindrances' of sensual desire, malevolence, sloth, distraction and doubt,[5] and to the inducing of the loftier spiritual qualities.[6] It was the hall-mark of religious 'distinction,'[7] and, when coupled with endeavour which was also *yoniso,* resulted in the winning of 'emancipation.'[8] From *yoniso-mana-sikāra,* as the root, springs joy, thence zest, thence composure, thence happiness, thence concentration; concentrated, we see and know things as they have become (*yathābhūtaṃ*); thus seeing and knowing, distaste arises, thence passionlessness, thence freedom.[9] *Yathābhūtaṃ* is constantly used to qualify verbs of cognition corresponding to the nouns given on the preceding page; and there is no doctrine or view of importance which is not declared to be thoroughly understood when it is 'known and seen,' discerned, comprehended, and so forth, 'as it really has become, by right insight.'[10] And that there was from the outset a *conscious* association between this phrase, as merely conveying emphasis, and the belief in Universal Becoming—a belief which finds formulation under the doctrines of Impermanence, Non-soul and Causal Genesis—appears clearly in the important 'Great Sutta of the Destruction of Craving.'[11] Here the Buddha is represented as rehearsing, in an emphatic and detailed catechism, the doctrine that mind (*viññāṇa*) has become (*bhūtaṃ*) through assignable conditions (in other words, that consciousness arises at any moment from a cause), and having come to be is liable to cease. And *'he who by right insight discerns this as it has become,'* or 'really,' can entertain no doubts as to whether mind is or is not perduring, immortal, and so forth.

That Buddhism was so seriously insistent on true or higher cognition being the apperception of things in a causal perspective, is due not to a genuinely scientific standpoint, but to its pragmatic earnestness. Its central theme was release from ill or *dukkha* through a right understanding of *dukkha*. It diagnosed in order to cure.

"How does one discern as-it-has-really-come-to-be both the genesis and the passing away of all dukkha-*phenomena?"*[12]

It may be judged that in this section we have strayed from psychological territory in discussing, not what Buddhists thought about 'knowing,' but what they thought about 'knowing well.' Rightly or wrongly, however, the inclusion has been done deliberately—*sampajāna.*

5. *Intuition, insight, supernormal consciousness*—The chief intellectual result in the concentrative exercises discussed above was a superlative clarity of mind; untroubled by either discursive intellection or hedonistic affection. Apart from any context, this might be read as a prescription for a rest-cure for overwrought minds, or as the pursuit of the ends known to philosophy as Quietism, Apatheia, Ataraxia. But the Jhāna-process, as met with in the longer Suttas, is usually found to lead up to no static poise of intellectual vacuity, but to a number of states, either serial, or alternative, of what may be called abnormal synergy—a term I follow Henry Maudsley in borrowing from medicine—so clearly is the state of consciousness said to be induced by voluntary intellection or will :

"With consciousness[13] *thus concentrated* [in Fourth, Jhāna), *made pure, translucent, cleared, void of defilement, made supple, wieldy, firm, imperturbable, he applies and bends-over the mind*[14] *to knowledge and vision."*

The possible alternative or serial states that might then be induced are described under eight heads, six of them being intuitive, and two being, if I may so say, kinetic:

(1) Discernment of the interrelation between body and mind[15] clearly revealed, as when the purity of a fine gem is being properly seen owing to its being threaded on a string.

(2) Supernormal hearing of sounds, voices, both human and celestial, the distant becoming near.

(3) Discernment of another person's consciousness.

(4) Reminiscence of former lives: "He recalls several previous sojournings, namely, one or more rebirths. . . in such a place such was my name. . . family. . . term of life. . . as if a man were to travel and, on coming home, should know where he had been and what he had done."

(5) Supernormal vision, or discernment of the destinies of beings deceasing and being reborn, "faring according to their deeds . . . just as a man from a balcony might watch persons entering or leaving the house, walking along the streets, seated at the cross-roads; and would know whither each was bound."

(6) Discernment and conscious extirpation of the influence of sense-desires, desire for rebirth, and of the mental obfuscation of ignorance. (These are likened to intoxicating drugs, or *āsăvăs,* and a fourth, speculative opinion, came to be added generally.) "As if from the bank of a mountain tarn of water, clear, translucent, serene, one were to look down and discern the shells, the fishes and the pebbly bottom."

(7) Evoking or creaṭing a phantom body (literally, 'made of mind'), the double of one's own body.

(8) Supernormal locomotion, or movements in which gravitation and opacity ceased to obstruct.

The last two are the usual phenomena of what, in Buddhist literature, is termed *iddhi,* a word meaning to stir, set in movement, and secondarily, to do so successfully, to have wrought. The second mode came to be called '*iddhi* by fixation of resolve' (*adhiṭṭhānā-iddhi*). No further record is here practicable of what these older texts say concerning them. It is only to be added that there was no belief in a 'soul' leaving the body temporarily, as the *jhāyin* sat 'rapt' in trance, or nearly so. We nowhere read of a comatose body, whose mental factors were arguing with angels, or elsewhere active. But it seemed to be claimed for the saint of old, that he had trained himself to such efferent power of synergy, that he could convert the momentary successions called *chitta* into body, or *vice vèrsa.*

Not even Buddhaghosa's account of *iddhi* and its induction is adequate to give us outsiders much insight into its working, or its psychology. Supernormal consciousness in genius or any other mode can only be testified to by the person so gifted, and must always elude self-analysis. Self-consciousness is necessarily at zero. The entire vitality, mental and bodily, is engaged in the making, the *poiēsis,* whether it be the synthesis of a new induction, the sympathy of aesthetic creation, or the synergy of super-normally adjusted action. The 'what' of experience is recollected, but not the 'how.' This holds for all the other six in the series.

With regard to reminiscence (4), cases of which, it has been claimed, occur, without *jhāna,* now and then in the East of to-day, among children, such an achievement may be as consistently upheld by a pious Buddhist, as by anyone who combined acceptance of it with belief in an immortal ego or soul. This may be made clearer in my concluding chapter. But with regard to the achievement of it by the adult consciousness of the Arahant or one nearly so, and only in Jhāna, Prof. Bergson's discussions on memory are strikingly suggestive.[16] Given our 'whole past ever about us' in the unknown spaceless working of mind in time, on which we cannot look back as we might, because life forces the forward view in us; given too the 'racial attention' to life grown weak, the desires and prospects in it interesting us no more, whether by impending death, *or from the deliberate renunciation of all they offer now and hereafter, as life*—can we not see that, in the light of this flooding in of the past for one who is ending life, and who is also convinced that his past includes infinitely many lives, his remembrance of that past becomes a lengthened vista? Such was the Arahant's (abnormal) lack of personal forward view on life; and who can say that his retrospect was not also abnormal?

Of these eight attainments in insight and will, numbers 2-

6 and 8 came to be known as the six super-knowledges (*abhiññā*). And on the whole body of them, the name of *vijjā* (Sanskrit, *vidyā*), or more usually *paññā*, was conferred,[17] more properly *paññā-kkhandha*, or body of intellectual (attainment). *Paññā*-vision, again, was of a wider or higher implication than the special supernormal 'vision:'

"The eye of flesh, the eye divine,
And eye of insight, best of all."[18]

And a fourth variety is sometimes mentioned: eye of truth, or insight into the nature of things.[19]

Nevertheless so protean and flexible is the term *paññā*, that it is used not only for intuitive knowledge, but for any exercise of intelligence, if only that intelligence is being *intelligently exercised.* The synonyms by which it is defined in the Abhidhamma-Piṭaka embrace nearly every aspect of cognition, from research and analysis to insight.[19] As a mental complex it is classed with the *sankhāra* aggregate; as a cognitive process it is thus compared with the more general term *viññāṇa:*

" *'What is it to have* paññā?' *'To discern* (pajānāti) *the method of the Four Truths.'* '*What is* viññāṇa?' '*Betng conscious, for instance, of pleasure or pain or neutral feeling.*' '*Are the two mutually involved or separate? And is it possible, considering them apart, to declare that they are different?' 'That is not possible; they are mutually involved. What one discerns, of that one is aware; of what one is aware, it is this that one discerns.' 'What distinguishes them then?'* 'Paññā *is to be developed;* viññāṇa *is to be understood.'"*

Feeling and perception are also stated to be bound up with, and not different from, *viññāṇa* or consciousness. Then:

"What is cognizable by representative consciousness (manoviññāṇa) *when it is detached from the five senses and attains entire clarity* (*i.e.* in the fourth stage of Jhāna)?"

The answer gives three of the four ulterior Jhānas enumerated above, pp. 117 f.

"And by what does one discern (pajānāti) *cognizable idea? By*

the eye of paññā. *But what is [here] the meaning of* paññā? Paññā *means higher knowledge* (abhiññā), *complete knowledge* (pariññā), *elimination* (pahāna)."[21]

"All are modes of knowing," comments Buddhaghosa, only the prefix differs. He then, by a simile which he much fancied,[22] compares *saññā, viññāṇa, paññā* to the different reaction provoked, at sight of the precious metals, in a child, a citizen, and a metallurgical expert. The first sees in them coloured objects; the second sees *also* in them tokens representing utilities to be got; the third is *also* able to judge as to their origin and their fashioner. Thus *viññāṇa* includes the work of perception and also general notions. But *paññā* includes both these, and also "by an uplift of energy attains to a revelation of the Way."

A Commentator was bound to be exegetical. But the concluding clause is a deeply interesting comment on the statement above: '*paññā* is to be developed.' The verb—*bhāvetabbā*—is literally must be made to become. It is constantly used in connexion with the meditative self-training of the Buddhist student. With it may be compared similar terms—*anubrūheti, vaḍḍheti,* develop, make to grow—used in connexion with mental culture.

"For it is through conditions, through a cause, that ideas arise and pass away. And by training certain ideas arise, others pass away."[23]

Such is the refrain in another dialogue already quoted.

In their arising is involved creative, constructive effort. And this is intuition or insight, that effort of "intellectual sympathy by which the mind can place itself within the mobile reality" of things.[24] *Paññā* was not simply exercise of thought on matters of general knowledge and practice, nor was it dialectic, nor desultory reverie. It was intelligence diverted by—or rather *as*—concentrated volition, from lower practical issues till, as a fusion of sympathy, synthesis, synergy, it 'made to become' that spiritual vision which had not been before.

We must now abandon this incomplete survey of the

extent to which the books, reckoned oldest in the Buddhist culture, analyse the nature of mental procedure. If we have found something, there is much we have not found—for instance, the image and the conditions of its reinstatement, an analysis of the emotions, instinct as compared with volition. We have now to see what later texts have done to make good any of these archaic silences.

References

1. *Dīgha-N.* iii. 219; *Saṃyutta-N.* v. 204; *Bud. Psy. Ethics,* pp. 86, 97.
2. *Yathābhūtaṃ* appears at least once in the *Mahābhārata* (iii 12070), which as a complete compilation is much later than the Nikāyas.
3. *Saṃyutta-N.* i. 203.
4. *Aṅguttara-N.* i. 87.
5. *Saṃyutta-N.* v. 85, 102; *Aṅguttara-N.* i. 5, 13.
6. *Ibid.,* i. 14.
7. *Dīgha-N.* iii. 273.
8. *Saṃyutta-N.* i. 105.
9. *Dīgha-N.* iii. 288.
10. Cp. the references in *Saṃyutta-N.* vi. 81, 82 (Index).
11. *Majjhima-N.* i. 260; cp. *Saṃyutta-N*. ii. 48.
12. *Saṃyutta-N.* iv. 188; *Aṅguttara-N.* i. 173 f.
13. *Dialogues,* i. 86 f.
14. Consciousness, mind= *chitta.*
15. *Viññāṇa.* The simile, of coure, illustrates not the interrelation, but the discernment.
16. Cp. *e.g.* his recent address: *Prceedings,* Psychical Research Society, 1913.
17. *Dialogues,* i. 124, 236; cp. 62, *n,* 1.
18. *Iti-vuttăkă,* § 61 (Fifth Nikāya). 'Eye divine' was the usual name for supernormal vision (3).
19. *Dialogues,* i. 95.
20. *Bud. Psy Ethics,* § 16.
21. *Majjhima-N.* i. 292 f.: diaogue, already quoted between Mahā-koṭṭhita and Sāriputta. See above, p. 52.
22. Used in three of his works.
23. *Dialogues,* i. 247 f.
24. Bergson, *Introduction to Metaphysics.* The relatively specialized function assignd by Buddhaghosa to *Viññāṇa,* as compared with *Saññā,* and as compared with the very general conception of it in modern Buddhist theory (cp. pp. 8, 18, 54), forms the subject of an inquiry among Burmese teachers now being prosecuted, in response to my questions, by Mr. S.Z. Aung.

7

Psychological Development in the Abhidhamma-Piṭaka

We have left scanty space for such a discussion. It must, however, be remembered that to analyse, or detach from their contingent occasions, the doctrines expressed in the Suttas is largely the work of this section of the Canon; hence we have been forestalling much of what had else awaited us. As to the rest, I propose to bring out a few points revealing work done on those doctrines as it was carried on in the School, and not by way of addressing the congregation, or conversing with the individual inquirer. Work so done is the subject-matter and method of the Suttas.

The keynote to the contents of this Piṭaka is both the summarizing, and also the working-in of the details of the doctrines committed to the Order in the Sutta-teaching. This is what we might have expected to find under the given circumstances. The day of the master-minds of the founders was too recent for their utterances to be considered objectively, much less critically, whence might have sprung development of theory. And that day had witnessed such a breaking away from current theory—from *diṭṭhi*, which was so largely coincident with *atta-diṭṭhi*, or *attavāda*, or *sakkāya-diṭṭhi*,[1] all names for the same sort of metaphysic—that we cannot wonder if constructive imagination was held tightly down to working out the legacy, whereof the Abhidhammika teachers were the first heirs.

The one exception to this sterility in development of theory is the 'system of relations,' the analysis, that is to say, of all the types of relations observable between phenomena. The immensely detailed analysis of these twenty-four relations, or doctrine of events as conditioned, occupies the last 'great' book called Paṭṭhāna, and lies outside our subject.[2] But even that exposition lacks concise theoretic discussion.

In the developed psychological detail, the following features are of interest:

1. *Development of introspective analysis*—In the first book of the Abhidhamma-Piṭaka we come immediately upon a great development in statement, of the type of mental analysis in the *Anupăda Sutta* noticed above.[3] Human consciousness has been schematized as experiencing now one, now another, of a certain number of *types* of contents.[4] These are divided under three heads, *viz.*: eight types or classes of good consciousness (*chitta*), and twelve of bad consciousness characterizing human beings, and supposed also to characterize, more or less, beings infra-human, and all *devas*, or angels, exclusive of (*a*) the remoter, more ethereal Brahma- or Rūpa-world, and (*b*) the entirely immaterial A-rūpa world. Thirdly, types of morally indeterminate consciousness. Here consciousness is analysed, not as causing-result, but as itself caused-result, namely, of bygone acts in this, or previous lives. As in most of these seven books, the method of exposition is catechetical throughout. And the absence, for all the questioning, of any attempt to set forth more than formulas and definitions, seems to betray how largely such a work must have been merely a mnemonic guide, and a book of reference for term and set phrase, in the hands of the exponent giving his oral lessons. The component *dhamma*'s, or mental phenomena, into which anyone of these psychoses or concrete momentary *chitta*'s is resolved, have increased more than fivefold above those named in the above-quoted Sutta. The probable reason is that in any given person each type of conscious unit may, at a given moment, show some only of the components. The

door is left open, for that matter, for yet other components to be distinguished and added to the typical list, as particular and not typical features.

"Now these, or whatever other incorporeal, causally induced dhamma's *there are on that occasion—these are good* (or bad) dhamma's."

And the Commentator, elaborating yet more, specifies nine such complementary components, *e.g.* of the first 'good thought.' One of these, thus relegated to a relatively contingent place, is *manasikāra,* 'work of mind,' rendered above 'adapted attention.' This 'work-of-mind,' writes Buddhaghosa, is synonymous either with the 'adverting' of each sense, or with the adverting of the ensuing *mano,* or it is to be conceived, with respect to object, as the confronting and linking mind with object, as a driver harnessing horse and chariot (*Atthasālinī,* 133). Later developments brought this factor to the front.[5] The distinction between a moment of consciousness, where attention is or is not previously prepared or adjusted, is, in these types, otherwise taken into account. Every alternate type or class, namely, is declared to be motivated. This does not imply that the types lacking this feature are spontaneous, due to chance. All consciousness was conditioned. It only implies that the preceding consciousness had adverted already to the object in question. The Commentary gives, as illustrations, the prompting of what we call first and second thoughts, and prompting by another. This emphasis on attention is repeated in the discussion on sense, and lends for us a noteworthy modernity to this ancient analysis.

I have already commented on the intrusion of such a practical category as 'good' and 'bad' in matter so peculiarly psychological as that of introspective analysis. The Pali words are as wide in practical scope as our 'good' and 'bad.' Goodness applied to mind connotes wholesomeness, virtue, causing welfare, skill, writes the Commentator; of these the fourth meaning does not apply, the other three do. The terms therefore are ethically used. But both ethics and psychology are for the Buddhist but phases, logical distinctions in that one and central doctrine of the Norm, or, as we should say, cosmodicy, which constitutes for him philosophy and religion indissolubly united. To be and do good was to put thought and action into line with eternal, universal law, under which certain types of *chitta* would inevitably be followed, later if not sooner, by certain consciously felt results in self and in others. 'Self,' as reaping, would be the resultant, not the identical, self who sowed.

Practically, in these curious old analyses, 'good' is used only in the sense of 'felicific,' or causing welfare.[6] The caused welfare, or resulting pleasant consciousness, wherever and whenever experienced, is reckoned as undetermined or neutral; it is not itself reckoned as being 'good,' or felicific in its turn, but is called undetermined, indeterminate, unmanifested, *a-vyākată*.[7] Of such states neither good nor bad, writes the Commentator, is declared. This developed theory of consciousness, judged to be neutral with respect to result, and distinguished only as effect of past consciousness, I have not found in the Nikāyas.

2. *Development of psychological definition*—This feature is the most valuable contribution made by the Abhidhammikas to the psychology of Buddhism. Of their three compilations dealing largely, or even wholly, with definitions, a great part of the contents consists of inquiries into the nature of a number of mental complexes. The definitions may not be satisfying to our own logical tradition. They consist very largely of enumerations of synonymous or partly synonymous terms of, as it were, overlapping circles. But they reveal to us much useful information concerning the term described, the terms describing, and the terms which we may have expected to find, but find not. And they show the Sokratic earnestness with which these early Schoolmen strove to clarify their concepts, so as to guard their doctrines from the heretical innovations, to which ambiguity in terms would yield cheap foothold.

As instances of the light thrown for us by this mass of conscientious cataloguing, we may note a few purely psychological definitions:

(i) *"Which are the phenomena that are* (a) *of the self,* (b) *external?*

"Ans. (a) *The spheres (fields) of the five senses and of mano* (sensus conlnlunis, *etc.*); (b) *the spheres of the five kinds of sense-objects and of mental objects* (dhammā)."[8]

"In what respect is this or that khandha (a) *of the self,* (b) *external?*

"Ans. (a) *That* khandha *which, for these or those beings, is of the self, is self-referable, one's own, referable to the person. . . .* (b) *That* khandha *which for these or those other beings, other persons, is of the self, is self-referable, their own, referable to the person.*"[9]

We have here the field of object including not only all that is directly presented to 'my' experience considered as the subject, but also all that is subjective for others. It would have been convenient to render (*a*) and (*b*) in the questions by subjective and objective. The pairs of terms, however, are not exactly parallel. *Bāhira, bahiddhā,* mean just 'external.' But the other term (*a*) is ampler than 'subjective,' including all the elements, abstractly conceived—extended, cohesive, etc.[10]—that enter into the composition of the individual. 'Subjective' often fits well, especially in the more academic developments of Abhidhamma, but for the Buddhist, as with us, 'self is a fairly fluid term.'[11] There was, for this philosophy, no academic dualism to accentuate and rationalize the popular antithesis, used in the Suttas, of body and mind. There was only on the one hand the fleeting mobile compounds that made up what it was convenient to call 'me,' 'myself,' 'this individual,' and, on the other hand, all compounds that were 'other,' external to that self. This was the only 'subjective-objective' distinction that was, and, I believe, has ever been, recognized.

(ii) *"What on that occasion is the power (or faculty) of mindfulness* (sati'ndriya)?

"Ans. *The mindfulness which on that occasion is recollecting, calling back to mind; the mindfulness which is remembering, bearing in mind, the opposite of superficiality and of obliviousness. . . this is the power of mindfulness that there then is.*"[12]

This term has been discussed above. I have added the Abhidhamma definition to make clear the comprehensiveness of its meaning. That, etymologically, is memory, or remembering; practically, it is clear thinking on past or present.

"Opposite of superficiality" is literally "state-of-not-floating,"—'like pumpkins and empty pots on the surface of water" is the comment—"but sinking on to the object of thought," and again "non-floating and apprehension (*upagaṇhănă*) are its essential marks." In it, consciousness reminds itself of what it has (its past being wrought up with its present), like a treasurer detailing his revenue to a king. Past, present, future, the threefold time-distinction, is constantly cited, but the problem of forgetfulness and reinstatement, and the conditions of reinstatement, usually alluded to among ourselves as association of ideas, are still not raised as matters calling for definition.

(iii) It is more in the Abhidhamma elaboration of sense-analysis that distinctions of time are brought forward. This analysis reveals an increase in precision of statement rather than in theory, or added matter of observation. But it remains the fullest experiential statement of sense-consciousness which ancient literature has given us. It occurs in the first book, and is included under the inquiry into material qualities in general or *rūpa.*[13] The four elemental material qualities are 'underived,' *no upādā,* or irreducible; the sense-organs, and all sense-objects, *except those of touch,* are derived, that is, from the underived elementals. Hence the ancient Hellenic theory that 'like is known by like' may be considered as latent in this arrangement,[14] although it is only in Buddhaghosa that I have found it made explicit: "Where there is difference of kind there is no stimulus. The Ancients say that sensory stimulus is of similar kinds, not of different kinds."[15]

Each of the five special senses, and then the *mano*, co-ordinator of sense, is set out in a fourfold formula, carefully worded and voluble as compared with the jejune statement of organ, object *plus* contact, of the Nikāyas. Summarized, the formula takes account of (*a*) the sense, invisible (the fleshy organ is not included) and reacting, (*b*) the object invisible also (as presentation) and impinging, and (*c*) the contact. Further,

(1) the fact of possible sensation;
(2) the actual impact of object;
(3) the actual impact of sense;
(4) the resultant actual impression and possible results in the four incorporeal aggregates.

The severance of (2) and (3) is explained by the Commentary as indicating (2) involuntary sensation, *e.g.* an unexpected seeing of lightning, and (3) voluntary seeing, 'looking,' for example, or 'listening'—adjusted movement of attention of "one who by his own wish, seeking to look at some object, concentrates his vision."

And in all four statements, there is the detailed time-reference—'has seen, sees, will or may see,' 'has impinged, impinges, will or may impinge.' Sense is emphatically stated—as an experience in time no less than in space. With sense 'purged,' everything becomes in a way 'present' to consciousness, 'bending over the present moment.'

(iv) *"What is that material quality which is not derived?* (a) *The sphere of the tangible;* (b) *the cohesive element. What is* (a)*? The extended, calorific and mobile elements; the hard, the soft, the smooth, the rough, pleasant contact, painful contact, the heavy, the light. . . . What is* (b)*? The watery or clinging element* [āpo], *the binding quality in [things] material."*[16]

I have alluded already (pp. 18 f.) to this philosophic abstraction of cohesiveness, etc., as superseding in Buddhist culture the more primitive category of the four (or more) elements. The salient feature in the cohesive element is fluidity, adds the Commentary. It is exempted from the tangible, inasmuch as that which is felt, in a concrete liquid, is the other three elements, *not* the cohesion of them. We feel its resistance, its heat or cold, its movement. And these three we apprehend through the most fundamental of our senses, namely, touch. The other sense-organs and objects are, relatively speaking, as cotton balls striking other cotton balls on the elemental anvils. But touch is as a hammer smiting through its cotton to the anvils (Comy.).

(v) *"Now on that occasion* (i.e. *at the genesis of the first type of good consciousness) there are the four (mental) 'aggregates.' . . . What on that occasion is the* sankhāra-kkhandha *(group of complexes)? Contact, volition, initial and sustained application, zest, concentrating ; the five moral powers—faith, energy, mindfulness, concentration, insight—; vital power, rightness of views, intention, endeavour, mindfulness, concentration; the forces of faith. . . insight (as above); the forces of modesty and discretion, disinterestedness, amity, understanding; no- covetousness, no-malice; composure, buoyancy, pliancy, fitness, proficiency, rectitude of consciousness and its properties, mindfulness and intelligence, calm and insight, grasp and balance—these, or whatever other incorporeal causally induced phenomena there are on that occasion, exclusive of the aggregates of feeling, perception, and of consciousness—these are the aggregate of sankhāra's."*[17]

The contents of this fourth aggregate are re-stated with the explication of each of the other types of good and of bad consciousness, the items varying according to the typical nature of the psychosis analysed. The next type, for example, lacking the intelligent or intellectual character of the first type, all the constituents implying understanding, insight, etc., are omitted, and so on.

This is a notable elaboration in what Croom Robertson used to call 'bodying out a thought,' as compared with the simple description of this particular 'group' in the Nikāyas. And it is intended to express, not what is present in consciousness at every flicker of the type evoked, but the field of choice, the range and potentiality, in the conscious activity ranked under the given type. These good and bad types of consciousness that are being analysed, are each and all said to be caused on occasion of a mental object, either a sense-impression, or a revived impression. And the contents of the mental complexes of an Ariya-sāvaka—a saintly student—would differ greatly from that of the average layman whom he taught, when some external object evoked in each the same type of consciousness.

Viewed in this way, the analyses are not so overdone as at first sight they seem to be. They are all in keeping with one of the chief tasks of the Abhidhamma compilers: the jealous guarding of the doctrines of the Suttas, in their oral preservation and transmission, from errors arising through vagueness and ambiguity of language. And thus it is that they have left us a mass of exponential detail with no exposition of theory. The doctrine (*Dhamma*) had been declared, learnt and handed on in set verbal forms. In *Abhidhamma* the teacher, conversant with the Dhamma, and teaching it in his turn, possessed, in the definitions of these seven supplementary books, a thesaurus of reference helping to clarify his knowledge and his expositions.

A curious feature in these seven Abhidhamma-books is the beginning of the distinction: *chitta* and *chetasika's*, which was finally to supersede in psychological analysis the more cumbrous khandha-division.

"Which are the mental phenomena that are (a) *of mind* (chitta)? . . . (b) *that are mental properties* (chetasikā)?"[18]

The first are stated to be the five kinds of sense-awareness (*viññāṇa*), the *mano*-element, and representative cognition. The latter comprise the aggregates of feeling, perception and *sankhāra*'s. *Chetasikā* and *chitta* have swallowed the five aggregates between them. In probably the latest Abhidhamma-book, *Kathā-vatthu,* we find a list of mental phenomena, greatly abbreviated by an 'etc.' in the middle, but evidently covering the three above-named aggregates, and called *chetasika*'s. These were to be regarded as the coexistent accompaniments—whether all or some of them is not yet stated—of *chitta.*

8. *Generalizing in matter and in form*—To a great extent, the doctrines as we have them in the oldest books were very largely enunciated *ad hominem,* as replies to particular inquirers, bringing particular needs to be satisfied, and special defects to be put right. Many also, it is true, were spoken *ad parisam, i.e.* to the *parisā,* or company of disciples. This was a variable quantity, as the many years and tours of the Founder's long life of mission work went on, and was so far different from the little nucleus named in the Christian gospels that it might, on any occasion, consist of a very mixed group of intelligences, from the novice, or the 'untamed' or untamable bhikkhu, up to men of intellect and extraordinary gifts like Sāriputta, and like Moggallāna and Kassāpa, both termed Mahā or Great. Such chosen followers were often touring, each with his own band of learners.

The Abhidhammikas set themselves to eliminate from the doctrines, thus adapted to individuals and small groups, all that was contingent in narrative; the episode eliciting the pronouncement, the comparative method of conveying its meaning, the parable and the simile, that appealed to this or that hearer. The bare judgn1ent, or predication, was thus registered, and its terms defined. The result is not attractive reading, but the purpose was doubtless served. Taken altogether we have, in Abhidhamma, not a well-constructed philosophical system, but all the materials for one. "The Dhamma," wrote the learned Ledi Sadaw in his essay on Abhidhamma, "is taught in two ways: in formulas suitable for memorizing . . . and in instruction imparted directly and specifically to individuals. By the former method the matter is analysed either in outline or in detail, without regard as to whether perplexities may arise or not . . . . Now the great field of Abhidhamma instruction is one of formulas, . . . wherein one must keep in view, not only those who are listening on anyone occasion, but the general course of the doctrine according to the meaning and the letter. Thus will the teaching make for increase of analytical knowledge in those Ariyan students who have learned the doctrines, and for the acquisition, some future day, of analytical knowledge by ordinary folk."[19]

But this elimination of what was contingent matter does not exhaust Abhidhamma generalizing. Had this negative work been all, we might have had the not-to-be-regretted result of a Piṭaka shorn of some of its length. By the logic of consistency or symmetry, the Abhidhammikas judged it right to apply their doctrinal formulas, psychological and otherwise, not only to normal humanity, but also to supernormal humans like the arahants, and to those companies of celestial beings on different planes of life, to which normal humans were, as religious beings, habitually aspiring.

We find the inquiry into normal human consciousness exacting enough, and consign the study of the abnormal and pathological mind to quasi-physiological treatises, and that of superhuman consciousness to theologians. We are adding the study of the infra-human animal mind to the by-products of our psychology, but only since yesterday. If we profess to include in that psychology an inquiry into all manifestations of co-nsciousness, we have become, in this last respect, more catholic in outlook than the Buddhists. Their *'satta'* is practically coextensive with our 'creature' or 'being.' And for them there is even less of any logical dividing-line between creatures, human, sub- and super-human, than our own tradition and prejudice reveal. Yet they, with a creed of pity and tenderness for *all* beings, have not extended their intellectual curiosity to the mental processes of those that were, as they held, temporarily undergoing an unhappy phase of life's unending pulsations. The wealth of sympathetic insight into animal life shown in the Jātaka tales, the belief that rebirth as aninlal was a fate very likely awaiting the foolish person you were addressing, if not yourself—

"Those who leave this world and are reborn as human beings are few, but those who. . . are reborn in purgatory, among beasts, among

the shades, are many"[20]—

make this omission somewhat strange. We only read that rebirth as an animal was considered as the result of a more or less immoral previous life while a human being, and as a life only less full of ill than the doom of purgatory. So greatly, no doubt, was the apparent joyousness of much animal life[21] overshadowed, for the sensitive and intellectual Indian, by the mercilessness of nature and of man of the one hand, and by the incapacity of the animal for attaining spiritual development, on the other.

"*There are these five realms of life* (lit. *goings*), *Sāriputta: purgatory, the animal kingdom* (lit. *matrix*), *the shade plane, mankind, the devas. And I understand* (pajānāmi) *purgatory, and the way that leads thereto, and the career through which, if practised, one is reborn after death to the dread doom of the Waste, the Downfall of the constant round. And I understand the animal kingdom, and the way that leads thereto, and the career, because of which one is reborn after death therein.*"[22]

The three remaining realms of life are declared to be understood by the Buddha no less, and so, he adds, is Nibbāna. But the Nikāyas contain no detailed revelation of that understanding so far as the first three realms are concerned. Concerning, however, the realm of devas—and this includes everything that we conceive as god, angel or guardian spirit, but not disembodied soul—the Abhidhammikas so generalize their psychological predications as to take the deva-consciousness sometimes into account. They considered that all men, except the arahants, were aspiring, well or badly, to be reborn as devas of some kind, to a larger, longer, serener life. There was no difference of *kind*, no presence or absence of soul, much less specific variety of soul,[23] to distinguish deva from either man or animal. All were creatures, conditioned, compound persons, adapted to this mode of life or that.

Now it seemed to the compilers of the Abhidhamma books, either a legitimate exercise of curiosity, or a useful exercise in deduction—perhaps both—to state how much of the five-aggregate composition might go to make up rebirth in this or that deva-realm. For instance:

"Where mutterial qualities (rūpa-kkhandha) are reborn, is *feeling there reborn? Ans. In the sphere of unconscious being the* rūpakkhandha *is reborn, but not feeling. In the realm of the five aggregates, both material qualities and feeling are reborn. But where feeling is reborn, are material qualities there reborn? Ans. In the invisible [or formless] world, feeling is reborn, but not 'material qualities.'*[24]

I have referred, in the book quoted, to the mass of catechism dealing with such matters as possibly an exercise in deduction, because it is fairly evident that when once the current doctrines, about the nature of life in other spheres than that of this world, were formularized, or at least definitely conceived, it could be deduced how far the personal compound inhabiting this earth would require modifying, in order to fit into this or that other sphere. The statements are not imparted as revelations, but as the explication of what ought to be; in the mind of an orthodox graduate, the conception of each class of beings; and of each plane of rebirth, in which he had been taught to believe. Hence, again, the statements are not drawn up as speculations. The founders of the doctrines 'understood' these spheres, because—so it was believed—they had 'seen,' beholding by the 'celestial eye,' the pageant of the rebirth and decease of the successive lives of an indefinite number of being. Like *theôroi* at the Olympic Games—no mere spectators, but, in the fuller sense of that term, sacred deputies—they were accepted as representatives to other men of godlike powers, believed to be not superhuman, but supernormal only.

References

1. *i.e.* theory of self or soul, doctrine or school of ditto, theory of

individuality.
2. But see pp. 194 f.
3. See pp. 96f.
4. *Bud. Psy. Ethics* (a translation of this book), pp. 1 ff.
5. See below, p. 176, and *Bud., Psy. Ethics,* 34, *n.* 1.
6. Cp. *Bud. Psy. Ethics,* Ixxxii. f.
7. So in Ceylon tradition. Burma and Siam write *abyākata.*
8. *Bud. Psy. Ethics,* § 1207 f.
9. *Ibid.,* § 1044 f.; *Vibhaṅga,* pp. 2f. The former work has *dhammā* for *khandha.* On *Khandha, i.e.* personal factor mental or bodily, see above, pp. 40f.
10. *Bud. Psy. Ethics,* § 597 f.; cp. *Majjhima-N.* i. 185 f., 421. f.
11. Cp. W. James, *Prin. Psy.* i. 292 f.
12. *Bud. Psy. Ethics,* § 14 *Sati* derives from *s*[*m*] *arati,* 'to remember.'
13. Translated in *Bud. Psy. Ethics,* pp. 172 ff.
14. Empedokels, Ploto, Plotinus, who accepted it, were all influenced, through Pythagorism or elsewise, by Eastern thought.
15. *Atthasālinī,* 313, cp. above, p. 67.
16. *Bud. Psy. Ethics,* §§ 647, 652; the renderings are slightly altered from those judged best fourteen years ago. Cp. *Compendium,* 232.
17. *Bud. Psy, Ethics,* 62.
18. *Bud. Psy. Ethics,* p. 318; *Dhātukathā,* pp. 38f. On the term in the Nikāyas, see *Compendium,* 239, *n.* 1.
19. *Yămăka,* ii, (P.T.S.), pp. 222, 29; translated in *JPTS,* 1914, pp. 116, 124.
20. *Aṅguttara-N.* i. 37.
21. Awareness of this in bird life is a pleasant detail in the Theras' poems; cp. *Psalms of the Brethren,* pp. 27. 153, 364, 379.
22. *Majjhima-N.* i. 73.
23. The Buddhist devas are like pious, intelligent human beings, now consulting or worshipping a superman, now admonishing a human fool.
24. *Yamăkă,* i. 19.

Note To p. 152, *n.* 2.—Mention might here have been made of a Buddha-discourse (*Majjh.-N.* iii 169), in which he speaks of the miseries of rebirth as an animal: "*And I might talk on in many ways, so hard is it adequately to state the ills of the animal world!*"

8

Psychological Developements in the Milinda

The Questions of King Milinda,[1] in its psychological discussions, affords us interesting glimpses of development in theory midway between the Nikāyas and the Commentaries of the fifth century. No one as yet has sifted the contents of the only other Theravāda works, reckoned as authoritative, which have survived from the centuries when Buddhism was contending with, and becoming infected by, heretics in India, and was becoming thoroughly established in Ceylon—I refer to the *Netti,* 'Leading' or 'Guidance,'[2] and *Peṭakopadesa.* In the *Milinda* we have the advantage of a fairly astute lay mind, bringing its problems and dilemmas to the orthodoxly trained mind of a genial and accomplished senior bhikkhu. The latter is apt, when pressed, to declare exceptions to a rule or law as practically proving, not *testing* it. But for the most part his replies are very illuminating, and reveal here and there developments in theory and exposition, to which the later scholastics show their indebtedness. Briefly summing up those that bear on our subject, we may notice the following:

The dialogue branches into a great variety of subjects, religious, ethical, monastic, philosophical, but it is occupied for some fifty pages (in the translation) with purely psychological matter, and for some fifty more with psycho-philosophical matter as to 'soul.'

One statement, not without interest here, is the measuring what we should call growth in holiness, graduation in saintship, in terms of increasing ability in intellection, or play of intellect.[3] The problem is how to reconcile the orthodox belief in the omniscience of the Buddha with the necessity of his having to consider (or reflect, *ā-vajjăna,* lit. ad-vert) before cognizing anything he wished. In reply, seven types of *chitta*'s are described, forming a scale in mental culture (*bhāvitattaṃ chittassa*) from the least trained up to the supremely trained or Buddha mind, *i.e.* of the supreme type of Buddhas, known from this time onward as *sabb'aññu,* omni-scient, who gave themselves to enlighten and help mankind. In each grade, the mind is described as being brought quickly and easily into play about a greater range of subjects, remaining stiff and sluggish in action about a diminishing range of subjects.

'Culture,' here, is the term 'make-to-be,' cause-to-become,' associated above with developed intelligence (*paññā*). Perhaps 'development' or 'evolution' is at least as fit a rendering. And the supreme type of mind is declared to be so 'evolved,' that its thorough knowledge concerning everything knowable is, at any given moment, and with respect to a given subject, either actual, or potential with a potentiality swiftly transformable into actuality. The scheme is interesting as showing both the importance of intelligence or intellect in the Buddhist scheme of religious values, and also the oneness in kind between all human intellect, even up to the intellect of those who were ranked above the gods.

Concepts of mental functioning are discussed much after the earlier fashion of the Nikāyas, and usually during the repudiation; by the sage, of the animistic position. Just as the latest of the books in the Abhidhamma-Piṭaka opens its reasoned refutations of heresies with a much-detailed argument against the existence of any individual entity, so does Nāgasena, answering to his name as his first reply to the king, declare 'himself' to be but a mere convenient label for a number of parts and aggregates. "For there exists no permanent entity."[4]

It is of historical interest that he here uses the opening phrase of the book just referred to and its term for entity or soul: not *attā*, but *puggala*. In fact, throughout his dissertations, terms other than *attā* are used: *puggala, jīva* (life, vital spirit),[5] *vedăgu*, sentient agent.[6] *Jīva*, in the Sānkhya school, is the empirical soul, the intermediary, so to speak, between the organism and the absolute or noumenal soul. And it would almost appear as if *attā* had, at least for a time, come to signify merely the personal appearance or visible self.[7]

The mental processes discussed are chiefly those to which attention was given in connection with the Nikāyas. But there are points of added interest.

The sage has replied that "if he die with natural desires still at work in him, he will be reborn, but if not, no." Milinda asks if through reasoned thinking one "is not reborn." Nāgasena: "Both by reasoned thinking, sire, by insight and by other good qualities." "But are not reasoned thinking and insight just the same?" "No, sire, they are different. Sheep and goats, oxen, buffaloes, camels, asses are capable of reasoned thinking, but not of insight."[8] Reasoned thinking and insight are then described by the respective essential features of mental grasp and elimination or severance, just as a reaper grasps with one hand and prescinds with the sickle.

'Reasoned thinking' and 'insight' are *yoniso-manasikāra* and *paññā*, discussed above (pp. 123, 130). We should have possibly named dogs, elephants, monkeys, for the beasts named above. But clearly, not the most intelligent animals are meant; merely 'animals' in general. Now, in the Nikāyas, the ability and habit of *yoniso-manasikāra* is the basis of all higher spiritual training. The English for it is not easy to find. Mr. Gooneratne has 'wise contemplation,'[9] which in the *Milinda* context were a misfit. The term may possibly have depreciated a little during the centuries. If not, the crediting of animals with it lends point to the anomaly, pointed out above, with regard to inquiry into the mind of animals.[10] The association of *paññā* with 'elmlination' dates from the Nikāyas, as we saw. It is, at the same time, exegetical, and not exhaustive of the import of the word. "Illumination," says the sage, a little later, "is also its mark. . . . It causes the splendour of wisdom to shine, it reveals the Āriyan truths. . . as a lamp brought into a dark house."[11] Again, like the wind, it has no abiding-place.[12]

Concerning the eight attainments called (p. 129 f.) *paññā-kkhandha*, or body of applied insight, the *Questions* refer to those known as super-knowledges (*abhiññā*'s), and frequent allusion is made to supernormal will (*adhiṭṭhānā-iddhi*), both as mere magic,[13] and again, as a power wielded by the saint,[14] and only limited should the still mightier result of past karma interfere with it.[15] In one passage the power is likened to that of the synergy of an athletic action:[16]

"Yes, sire, there are persons who can go with this four-element-made body to Uttărăkuru or to Brahma-world; or to any other part of this world." "But how can they?" "Do you admit, sire, having ever jumped three or six feet of ground?" "Yes, sir, I do; I can jump twelve feet." "But how?" "I cause this idea (*chitta*) to arise: 'there will I alight!' With the genesis of the idea my body becomes buoyant to me." "Just so, sire, does a bhikkhu, who has *iddhi* and mastery over *chitta*, lifting up the body in consciousness, travel through the air by way of *chitta*."

Again, when Milinda is puzzled how a bhikkhu, who has will and mastery over mind, can vanish, and reappear in the Brahma-world, which is supposed to be distant a four-months' journey of a falling body from the earth, "as soon as a strong man could stretch forth and bend in again his arm," he is asked to think of anything he ever did at his birthplace (Alasanda = Alexandria, in Baktria), two hundred leagues away. He does so. "So easily, sire, have you travelled so far?"[17] comments the sage, likening will-locomotion to thought.

Reverting to the insight-faculty itself, the following distinctions are less encumbered by exegetical metaphor:

"These three: consciousness (*viññāṇa*), insight (*paññā*), and the soul (*jīva*) in a creature—are they different in meaning as well as in the letter, or do they mean the same, differing only in the letter?" "Awareness, sire, is the mark of consciousness, and discernment, of insight; there does not exist a soul in beings."[18]

This is a close approximation to the question discussed above from the Nikāyas.[19] And the eighteenth-century translator of the *Questions* into Singhalese amplifies the passage with a borrowed and condensed version of Buddhaghosa's comment and parable, to which I have referred. *Paññā* (Sk. *prajñā*), be it noted, was identified, by the older Upanishads, as none other, ultimately considered, than the Ātman itself: 'base and guiding principle of all that is.' Modified as *jīva*, the *attā* was shorn of its pantheistic import, and was more akin to the individual soul familiar to our own tradition. But, to pursue this psycho-philosophical question a. little farther, the soul, as *jīva*, or *vedagu* (knower), was still conceived as a willentity or agent, who, were he immanent, would, in order to *know*, not need to act through the intermediacy of the different channels of coming-to-know, to wit, the five senses and the *sensus communis* or co-ordinating, internal *mano*.

"What is this, sire, the 'soul' (*vedagu*)?"

"The life [-principle] (*jīva*) within, which sees through the eye, hears through the ear. . . and cognizes phenomena through mind, just as we, sitting here in the palace, can look out of any window we wish, east, west,- north or south." . . . "If this *jīva* acts as you say, choosing its window as it likes, can it not then see through anyone of the five senses, or so hear, so taste, etc?"[20]

And later :

"But if, sir, there be no such thing as a soul, what is it then which sees objects with the eye, hears sounds with the ear, . . . or perceives objects with the mind?"

The Elder said: "If the soul does all this, then [it would not need the specialized apparatus of each sense] it would see, hear, etc., more clearly if the sense-organ were removed; but it is not the case that we see, hear, etc., better if the eye-aperture, etc., has the organ removed; hence there is no agent in sensation independent of the specific functioning of each sense."[21]

This argument, with its analogy of choice of window in contemplating the external world, is much on all-fours with that, in the Nikāyas,[22] of the *attā* exercising arbitrary will as one or other of the aggregates, so as to modify the personal present fate and

"remould it nearer to the heart's desire."

The form of animistic philosophy, against which it is a protest, may well have been the *jīva* theory of the Sānkhya-Sūtras. This was but a convenient fiction or schema, by which the else inconceivable action of the noumenal soul, called *purusha* (an equivalent of *puggala*), *ātman*, or *kevala* (absolute), upon body, sense and *mano* might be expressed in words. Thus the *purusha* was indifferent, impassive, separate; the senses acted mechanically. But sensation became conscious life when *jīva* glowed in it, like fire in hot iron, or as a red blossom in a crystal, the *purusha* losing nothing thereby.[23]

The really important point that arises out of this, at first sight, somewhat futile argument of Nāgasena, is his immediately following enunciation of natural law in mental procedure, wherein lay the main support of his case. He first emphasizes the fact (briefly stated in the Nikāyas) of the orderliness in sense :—we cannot taste with the stomach, or the external skin; each channel of sense has its own procedure. The king is then made to ask whether a sense-impression always has *mano*-consciousness (co-ordination of sense) as its concomitant. "Yes." "Which happens first?" "First the sensation, then *mano* functions." The king asks whether sensation induces this perceiving by an injunction, or whether perception bids sense to supervene. The reply is, there is no such intercourse; the sequence happens through

(1) 'inclination' or natural tendency, (2) existing structure, (3) habitual process, (4) practice. These conditions are severally illustrated by similes: (1) by rain-water running away according to natural *slope*; (2) by the one means of egress and ingress used in a walled city; (3) by the usual order observed by the waggons of a caravanserai—first waggon second waggon, etc.; (4) by the arts of writing, arithmetic and valuation, skill succeeding clumsiness. through association set up by practice.

It was this *cosmos*, without and within, evident if not to be accounted for, that Buddhism accepted, as a saner, better-based view of things than that of the antinomy of an entity or soul, associated with the organism and yet not of it, and therefore, as the Kaiser Sigismund said of himself, super *grammaticam*, that is, *super* that organism's *grammaticam*.

Further discussions on mental process yield some more definitions. The other concomitants of the happening of a mano-consciousness, beside the 'contact' on occasion of sense (between sense and its object), are stated to be feeling, perception, volition, onset of and sustained attention. These amount practically to the four immaterial aggregates, and are to be understood as the contents of a state or process of consciousness on occasion of sense. 'Contact' is illustrated by two rams butting, two cymbals clashing.[24] But, as we shall see, the *wherewithal* in the collision does not seem to have been conceived as matter in the case of sight and hearing. 'Feeling' is well described as 'the being experienced and the being enjoyed.' The character of 'perception' is cognizing—becoming aware, *e.g.* of visible objects, that is, of colours (Buddhist psychology still assigning only colour to bare visual impression). Thus a king's steward, visiting his treasure-house, perceives the variously coloured treasures. 'Recognizing' is a possible rendering, but in the term (*saññā*) the corresponding prefix is lacking.

'Volition' receives a definition of some interest. In the Abhidhamma-Piṭaka it is described by mere derivatives, throwing for us no light on its connotation. This is not far amiss if the term mean bare volition, or conation, since we have here an, or shall I say the, irreducible element of mind. Now the function or mark of volition, in these *Questions,*[25] is declared to be twofold: (1) deponent, and (2) causative; to wit, (1) thinking (or being caused to think), and (2) concocting or devising (to give effect to the thought). "As a man might prepare, concoct a poison and drinking it, give it also to others to drink." This dual idea was maintained up to Buddhaghosa's time. By him it is likened to the working and making to work of a peasant-farmer, and of a master-craftsman. And he applies the orthodox fourfold definition of his time to the term *(chetanā),* showing it to imply 'being made to think,' 'effort,' 'fixing,' 'arranging.'[16] It would therefore seem to be the motor element in consciousness with the further implication of direction or purpose, and may thus be better rendered by volition than by conation. The latter, as bare reaching out, or activity put forth, is referred to an *indriya-i.e.* a power or faculty analogous to the sense-powers, and called *viriya.* It is thus described in the Abhidhamma-Piṭaka :

> *"The mental inception of energy. . . the striving and onward effort, exertion and endeavour, zeal and ardour, vigour and fortitude, state of unfaltering effort, of sustained desire, of unflinching endurance, the solid grip of the burden."*[27]

All this, on the other hand, suggests rather an aspect of the whole consciousness and character (habitual potential consciousness) at any given moment. In such terms as *chetanā,* the effort is being made to dissever, in a psychosis, all the nuances that go to make up the complex of consciousness.

The twin terms initial and sustained mental application recur.[28] In the *Questions,* they are likened to *(a)* a carpenter fixing a shaped plank into a joint, and *(b)* the reverberations of the *(a)* blows dealt in shaping a metal pot: *(a)* is the applied attention, *(b)* repeated pulsations of attention thus directed.

This analysis of consciousness ends with a reflection on the difficulty of "fixing all those mental phenomena involved in a single impression, on occasion of sense, telling that such is contact, such feeling, etc.," as if a man in the Bay of Bengal were to taste the water and say in which river the drops had originally come down[29]—a metaphor quoted, as we saw, by Buddhaghosa. The factors were distinguishable, but not experienced as isolated, no more than the many flavours enjoyed in the sauce blended by Milinda's chef.[30]

The term *sati,* or mindfulness, is twice discussed; the second occasion suggests a later development, almost identifying the word with mindfulness of the past, or memory, and offering the earliest approach to a theory of association of ideas existing in Indian literature. Stating that *sati* arises both through inward perception and external signs, the sage is asked: "In how many ways does *sati* spring up?"[31] Seventeen ways are enumerated, but they fall properly into the two above-named groups, with the exception of two. These two amount to a statement of our own 'association by way of similarity and of contrast,' and apply of course to subjective experience in general, whether presentative or representative. "*Sati* arises," we read, ". . . from similarity. . . or difference of appearance. . . as on seeing one *like* her we call to mind the mother. . .," or remember that such a colour, sound, etc., is *different* from that of a certain thing. The other 'modes by which mindfulness arises' are carelessly strung together, and only deserve mention because, so far as I know, there is no other inquiry of the same date to place beside the list. Briefly, then, recollection by purely representative effort is said to be effected by direct intellection *(abhijānana),* by discursive volition, by the , making-to-become' of trained intuition in 'super-knowledge,' *i.e.* in remembering one's own former lives, and, lastly, by ordinary revival of past experience as compared with present thoughts. This is more especially effected when that experience was of a striking nature, causing deep emotion. Milinda would recollect easily his coronation, Nagasena his conversion; both would easily recall a pleasant or a painful episode. External suggestions of a visible or audible nature are also enumerated. The subject is then dropped.

Not less psychologically interesting is the exposition of a theory of dreams.[32] The physical conditions of dreaming are stated to be: firstly, the constant condition of 'monkey sleep,' that is, of a state between waking and deep sleep; secondly, the variable antecedents of morbid health, biliousness for instance. The other kind of antecedent, through which alone the dream has any relation to impending occurrences, is deva-influence or deva-induction. The meaning or object of this 'celestial' *(dibba)* intervention is accepted as current lore without criticism. As telepathic procedure, where the agency was of a physically more ethereal, or mentally less *canalized* composition than the recipient's mind, the occurrence would not seem supernatural to an Indian. It is added that the dreamer would not read the sign; he would relate, and an expert would interpret—a 'wrong means of livelihood and low art,' according to the ancient teaching of the Founder.[33]

In deep sleep the consciousness *(chitta)* is stated to have 'gone into,' that is, become one with the *bhavanga,* or flow of organic life, and 'does not go on,' 'does not recognize or discern what is pleasant or unpleasant. For consciousness, in this merely potential state, not being a continuum,[34] or persisting being, is practically non-existent. To what, if any, extent the life-flow moments include moments of what we now term subconscious mental life, I have yet to learn.

References

1. See Bibliography.
2. Edited by E. Hardy, P.T.S., 1902.
3. *Questions of King Milinda,* i. 154 f.
4. *Kathā-vatthu,* i. 2 (P.T.S. ed.); *Questions,* i. 40.
5. *Ibid.,* 48, 86, 132.
6. *Ibid.,* 86.
7. See above, p. 27; in the translation *attā* in translated by 'image.'
8. *Questions,* i. 50.
9. Translation of *Aṅguttara-N.* parts i. -iii, Gale, 1913.

10. P. 151.
11. *Questions,* i. 61.
12. *Ibid.,* i. 120.
13. *Ibid.* ii. 94.
14. *Ibid.,* ii. 231, 234, 259.
15. *Ibid.,* i. 261 f.
16. *Ibid.,* 130.
17. *Questions,* i. 126.
18. *Ibid.* i. 136.
19. See pp. 130ff.
20. *Questions,* i. 86.
21. *Questions,* i. 133.
22. See above, p. 31.
23. Cp. R. Garbe, *Sānkhya-philosophie,* pp. 305f.; *Sānkhya. Sūtras,* Nos. 99, 356. In Jain doctrine, it is the soul (*jīva*) the is 'coloured' (H. Jacobi, *Trans, Hist. Religions Cong.,* Oxford, ii. 63.
24. *Questions,* i. 92 f.
25. *Questions,* p. 94.
26. *Visuddhi-Magga,* ch. x.
27. *Bud. Psy, Ethics,* § 13.
28. Above, p. 89.
29. *Questions,* i. 133.
30. *Ibid,* i. 97. It became nevertheless orthodox doctrine to hold, that no two *chitta*'s of sense-reaction could arise at the same moment. There was swift succession and apparent simultaneity. Ledi Sadaw, *JPTS,* 1914, 149.
31. *Questions,* i. 21–23.
32. *Questions,* ii. 157.
33. *Dialogues,* i. 17.
34. See *Questions,* ii, 159, *n.* 2. Through Mr. S.Z. Aung's work on the *Compendium of Philosophy,* we are now in a better position to translate this passage.

9

Some Mediaeval Developments

Scanty space remains to discuss, even in outline, the additions and modifications made in mediaeval and modern Theravāda psychology. Nor is the time for such discussion yet fully arrived. Of the two chief fields awaiting further research—the works of Buddhaghosa and those of Anuruddha and his commentators—only a small fraction is yet edited in Roman letter, and only one work, the digest called *A Compendium of Philosophy,* dating from probably the twelfth century, is yet translated. The date of Buddhaghosa is eight centuries earlier. These two groups of literature, the one supplementing the other, represent the dominant influence in Theravāda philosophical (including psychological) thought up to the present day. S.Z. Aung writes that the modern Burmese view, excepting certain independent critiques made by Ledi Sadaw, is one with the teaching of Buddhaghosa and Sumangala[1] (author of the most authoritative commentary on the *Compendium).*

Thus much can at any rate be said merely by reading the titles in these groups: the original zest with which philosophic and religious thought occupied itself with psychological analysis has never faltered. The human being, with or without the variations deducible in celestial being, has remained, according to Theravāda Buddhism, the proper study of mankind.

Another notable writer, two of whose works are, extant, is about to become accessible to Europe, as far as publication in our own script makes him so. This is Buddhadatta, a contemporary of the more famous Buddhaghosa. The Rev. A.P. Buddhadatta of Ceylon has prepared an edition of his notable namesake's *Abhidhammāvatāra,* an 'introduction' to philosophy. In one respect, at least, he represents, perhaps better than Buddhaghosa, the earlier type of the classification with which we started in our first chapter.

Thus whereas Buddhaghosa expounds his psychology in terms of the five-aggregate division, Buddhadatta opens his scheme with the fourfold division of the *Compendium*—viz. mind, mental properties, material quality, Nibbāna.[2] He writes in metrical Pali, stopping at times to supply his own prose commentary: "*Chitta,* that is, being aware of what is within one's range. . . minding everything inclusively; one's own life-continuum." And later: "*Chetasika*'s, that is, conjoined with *chitta,* or becomings-*in-chitta (citte bhavā).* These also, like *chitta,* form the subject to object, as such forming a single class. As resultants or non-resultants in consciousness, they are divisible into two classes. As productive of good or bad result or neither (literally: as good, bad or indeterminate) they form three classes. As belonging to consciousness concerned with mundane experience, with rebirth in worlds of sublimated matter, with rebirth in immaterial worlds, and with subjects whence all rebirth-concerns are rejected, they form four classes."

He then enumerates all the 'mental properties' to be distinguished in analysing that first type of a good and happy thought or *chitta* on occasion of sense, detailed in the Abhidhamma-Piṭaka, and discussed in an earlier chapter (pp. 136, 145). He also introduces the important distinction, not brought out in the old original analysis, of some mental properties being constants *(nĭyătă)* and some contingent or occasional. "These five: pity, sympathy-with-joy, aversion from evil in act, speech and life, are inconstant; they arise sometimes (in such a type of consciousness]."

This distinction is clearly worked out in the *Compendium.* We cannot yet compare Buddhadatta and Buddhaghosa.

But the later *Compendium* shows clearly that, at all events, for psychological analysis, the 'five-groups' system has fallen into the background, and consciousness is resolved into *chitta* and its coefficients of *chetasika*'s, some of which are constant coefficients, and some of which are, in any given moment of consciousness, present, some not.

This, in the *Compendium of Philosophy,* is much better worked out than in the older writer. We there see that, in such a given moment, mental analysis declares to be distinguishable factors, or nuances, seven constant coefficients, the Pali for 'constant' being 'all-consciousness-common-to.' These are contact, feeling, perceiving, volitional intellection, individualization, [the accompanying awareness of] psychic life, attention. Without these there can be no supraliminal consciousness. Besides these there may or may not be distinguishable six occasional coefficients, the Pali for 'occasional' being, in Buddhadatta, not-fixed, not certain *(a-niyāta),* in the *Compendium,* 'scattered' *(pakiṇṇaka),* distributed. These are initial and sustained application,[3] deciding, effort, zest, desire-to-do, or intention.

These thirteen, the later work adds, are all neutral, morally speaking; they combine with other factors of consciousness which are distinguishably good or bad 'implicates' of *chitta.*

Such then is the evolution of this dual category. First, *chitta* only; with the stray mention of *chetasika,* singular in number, in one Nikāya. Then a group word only—*chitta-chetasika dhamma*'s, in the books of the (later) third Piṭaka. Then the second term, now plural, appears as a list in the latest book of that Piṭaka. Then the two terms described as separate philosophical categories in the fifth century, with fuller treatmient, finally, of the latter category, in the twelfth-century manual. And in that manual the five aggregates are enumerated but once, in a philosophical, not a psychological section, just to paraphrase the ancient term *nāma-rūpa* (mind-and-body),[4] before they are again and finally let go.

That a positive, if a very slow, evolution in psychological specialization is here to be seen, seems fairly clear. It may not be admitted in centres of Abhidhamma learning. I am not sure that the habit of regarding matters historically, so new as yet in our own world of science, is cultivated there. The theory of *chitta* and its properties or coefficient *chetasika*'s, in this or that group of conscious syntheses, is pursued in the *Compendium* with a good deal of very arid and to us also sterile numerical summarizing—an aftermath, I am tempted to think, of the so long preponderant booklessness in Indian culture. More instructive, and revealing a more notable development in analysis is the doctrine of function *(kiccha)* and of process *(vīthi, pavatti)*. And here whereas the *Compendium* reveals advance in summarization, it is in Buddhaghosa and Buddhadatta that, at present, we detect the original sources of its evolution.

In discussing the fifth *aggregate—viññāṇa,* or consciousness in its typical sense of coming-to-know, cognition,—Buddhaghosa enumerates fourteen modes *(ākārā)* in which there is *viññāṇa*-process,[5]—*viz.* at reconception, in subconsciousness (sleep, etc., *bhavanga),* in *ad-verted* attention *(ā-vajjana),* the five modes of special sense-impressions, recipience [of the same], investigation, determination, complete apprehension, and registration, and finally, at death. "At the end of registration, procedure is once more *bhavanga* (unconscious or subconscious). Then when *bhavanga* is again cut across, the course of consciousness having again acquired [the necessary] antecedents, adverting recurs, and so on, there being repetition of this procedure by way of the natural law *(niyămă)* of consciousness, until the *bhavanga* perishes. In each new life *(bhava,* literally becoming), the lapsing of the last subconscious *chitta* is called decease *(chuti,* falling). . . . But from decease [comes] again conception, and from conception again *bhavanga*—such is the procedure in the unarrested consciousness-continuum of beings faring on through eternity. But whoso attains Arahantship, to him when consciousness has ended, renewed birth and death have also ceased."[6]

The eleven modes of the cognitive process are briefly

described previous to this passage. But they have not the appearance of being stated for the first time. No explanation of them *as process* is judged necessary. And since Buddhadatta, in the fourth chapter of the work referred to,[7] also names these fourteen modes of *chitta,* it is probably right to conclude that they both were but handing on an analytical formula, which had evolved between their own time and that of the final closing of the Abhidhamma-Piṭaka.

But the exposition of the cognitive process is more clearly and concisely stated in the later *Compendium.* However swiftly an act of sense-perception may be performed, it was held that, in every such act, seventeen moments or flashes (the metaphor is mine) of consciousness took place, each moment being considered to involve the three time-phases of all 'becoming,' namely a nascent, static and dissolving phase. "Hence," we read, "the process [of sense-cognition] is thus: When, say, a visible object, after one *chitta*-moment (1) has passed, enters the avenue [or focus] of sight, the life-continuum *(bhavanga)* vibrating twice (2) (3), its stream is interrupted, then the adverting moment rises and ceases (4). Immediately after there arise and cease, in order, the visual impression *(viññāṇa),* aware of just that visible object (5), recipient consciousness (6), investigating consciousness (7), determining or assigning consciousness (8), then seven flashes of full perception," or apperception *(jăvăna)* (9-15); finally, *if* the percept is sufficiently vivid, two moments of retention or registering consciousness (16, 17). This phase etymologically is very differently named: *tad-āramaṇa,* or *that*-object—that and not another. "After that comes subsidence into the life-continuum."[8]

The later commentaries illustrate this multiple, if momentary, psychosis by the following simile: A man in deep sleep with covered head beneath a mango tree (stream of unconscious life or *bhavanga).* A wind stirs the branches (preceding *chitta* 1 and vibrating *bhavanga,* 2, 3). This causes a mango to fall by him (arrest or disruption of unconscious life). The man is waked by the falling fruit (adverting, 4). He uncovers his head (sense-impression of fruit, 5), picks up the fruit (receiving, 6), inspects it (investigaing, 7), determines what it is (determining, 8), eats it (full perception, 9-15), swallows the last morsels (registering, 16, 17), re-covers his head and sleeps again (subsidence into *bhavanga)*. ('After-taste' had perhaps been more apt for 16, 17.)

Such is the type of procedure where the impression is vivid. With fainter impressions, inception may take longer, or there may be no process of registering, whence comes retention and reproduction. There may even be no moments of full cognition, or, in the faintest stimuli conceivable, no sens-eimpression, but mere momentary *bhavanga-chalăna, i.e.* organic 'vibration.'

This is certainly, in its meticulous analysis, its so to speak microscopical introspection, a considerable elaboration of the simple Sutta statement, quoted in a former chapter, of *mano* as the resort of, and the indulger in, all the impressions of the special senses.[9] Nevertheless, the validity of that statement is piously upheld by Buddhaghosa, when he is discoursing on *mano.* This is in his Commentary on the first Abhidhamma Piṭaka book, a work containing better psychological matter than the more normative treatment of the *Visuddhi-Magga.* The work of *mano* is there explained in reference to that passage.

Quoting it, he goes on: "Those objects which are the field and range of the five senses are also enjoyed by *mano.* . . . Each object (colour, sound, etc.) enters the focus [of consciousness] by two doors or gates. The object of sight, for instance, when it becomes the condition of *bhavanga*-vibration, by striking on the visual organ, at that instant comes into the focus of the *mano*-door. Just as a bird coming through the air and alighting on a tree, at the same moment shakes a bough and casts its shadow on the earth, even so is the simultaneity of sense-stimulus and *mano*-access." Then follow adverting of *mano* and the rest of the process. But in work of *mano*-door only, there is no sense-impact. This is when, on a later occasion and being no matter where, we recall some previous sense-experience—the sight of the beautifully decorated shrine, the pleasant voice of the preacher, the odour of votive wreaths, the meal enjoyed with colleagues. Or we may, when lying on a hard bed, recall a soft, easy couch enjoyed at such a time. Thus to the adverting *mano* the tangible object seems to enter the door of touch, and to make the pleasant contact present. But there is no such impact at the time."[10]

Later on, the *mano*-element ('element' as being 'empty of substance' or 'entity') is described as "*following* the sense-impression, as having the essential mark of cognizing sights, sounds, etc., the property of receiving the same, the resulting phenomenon of truth (literally: thusness), and as its proximate antecedent, the vanishing of the sense. impression. . . ."[11] Its physical basis is the heart, and although the door-objects, which are not similarly bound, pass on, this is the *locus,* this has the function of receiving them. The investigating moment and the rest come under that developed activity of *mano* termed 'element of *mano*-consciousness,' and correspond more or less to what our text-books call representative cognition, much of which is always implicit, if perhaps latent, in an act of sense-perception. And where the work of mind is not largely automatic, and swiftly determined and apperceived, as on most occasions of sense, but is dealing with unfamiliar and problematical assimilation, we may presume that Buddhaghosa would admit that *chitta*-moments, predominantly of investigating, determining, etc., might be indefinitely multiplied. Unfortunately he has left us no work devoted entirely and systematically to mental analysis. And if there be any such later work by another hand, it is not yet accessible.

A complete exposition of this Commentary, however, would reveal much more incidental psychological matter of interest. For instance, it does not pause to point to anything problematical in the phenomenon of contact on occasion of sense, either in the physical necessity, except in touch, of a medium, or in the apparent anomaly of *rūpa* in contact with that which is *a-rūpa* (matter with mind). And it makes no dogmatic statement concerning this. Nevertheless remarks are let drop guarding the psychological position. Thus: "Eye impinges on visible object *(rūpa)* only means eye receiving the mental object *(ā-rammaṇa).*"[12] Again, when he alludes to the *Milinda* similes for contact—the rams butting and cymbals clashing—Buddhaghosa justifies the use of 'impact' as between consciousness and mental object only in the sense of attaining, achieving *(sampatti).*[13] And, generally speaking, the cause of feeling lies in the nature of consciousness itself, "just as the heat of melting lac is in its own tissue though ascribed to burning coal without."

There is a great deal more sagacious psychological comment scattered thickly up and down this Commentary, and to some extent the following Commentary on the *Vibhanga,* or second book of the Abhidhamma-Piṭaka.[14] Some day, in a separate monograph, the psychology of Buddhaghosa will take its lawful place in the history of psychology. It is as yet premature to attempt a digest of the contribution made by him. A good deal of this cumbers the pages of the older work translated in my so-called *Buddhist Psychological Ethics,* but imperfectly and incompletely presented. I will only quote two more remarks given there, to show, by these alone, how unworthy of a truly catholic perspective it will be, to take account of Aristotle's psychology and not of Buddhaghosa's when made accessible.

The 'work translated' just mentioned *(Dhamma-sangăṇi)* has replied to its query: "What is included under visible object?" by stating, first, colours, then forms of magnitude. On these the Commentary remarks: "Here, inasmuch as we are able to tell, 'long,' 'short,' etc., by touch, while we cannot so discern 'blue,' etc., therefore long, short, and so on are not to be taken as visual objects without explanation. It is only by customary usage that we can speak of anything as *visible* object which appears as long or short, great or small, etc. etc., when so placed as to compare with something else."[15] This may not bring us up to modern psychology, but it is a farther step towards Berkeley's rather one-sided view, that whenever we are seeing, we are really, in mind, touching, than is Aristotle's mere hint: "There is a movement which is perceptible both by touch and sight."[16]

Once more, in commenting on the question: "What is included under the organ of touch?" he writes:

"The organ of touch (literally, the material organic compound, or body, *kāya)* is diffused over the whole bodily form just as moisture pervades an entire cotton rag. With the exception of this quality of unspecialized organ, the sense ranks with the others. To the objection that, if the sensitive surface be so general, it would convey confused impressions, the reply is that, without this extensity, we should not get all the touch-differentiations that we do get. In an ultimate sense the organ of touch is both everywhere and not everywhere. Not everywhere to the extent of being in things as seen or as tasted, etc. We cannot segregate sensations as we can grains of sand: hence qualities appear to, but do not really, coalesce in the obj ect."[17]

Leaving the field of sense-cognition, another noteworthy contribution by Buddhaghosa is his recording what was probably the current development of the meaning of the term I have rendered as 'zest' *(pīti)*. This word in the canonical books is usually associated with either *sukha,* pleasant, happy feeling, or *pamōjja,* joy, gladness, and it was very generally rendered by 'joy.' Mr. Aung has strongly maintained that it is not so much an emotional as an intellectual quality, and, at least at its lowest power, stands for 'interest.' Thus the 'interest' of pursuit as compared with the *sukha* of realization is, by Buddhaghosa, likened to the thirsty heated traveller's quest compared with his reaching water, shade and rest.

But if *pīti* be not emotional, it is unmistakably emotion. 'Elnotional' is, has to be, used as the adjective of feeling. And *pīti* is classed, not with feeling *(vedanā-kkhandha),* but among the coefficients of consciousness called *sankhāra's* or *chetasika*'s. It is not simply pleasurable feeling *(sukha)*. But neither is emotion to be so defined. Emotion is feeling accompaliying an idea, the being 'moved' with a coefficient of representative consciousness. The canonical description of *pīti* allies it with terms of gladness, mirth and enthusiasm.[18] Buddhaghosa gives, as its essential features, the being pleased, expansion, and elation.[19] He also gives us the five grades of *pīti:* the thrill of eagerness, the momentary flash, the flood of enthusiasm, as waves breaking over us, ecstasy or transport, and rapture. And all the instances given refer to an idea or group of ideas as the proximate cause. Hence whereas no one word need suffice, 'joy' as the more exultant, uplifted form of interest or zest is by no means always a mistranslation. And as the Commentary on the *Psalms of the Sisters and Brethren* renders by *pīti-sukha* their emotion on reviewing their own struggles to the goal, so do I judge that Buddhaghosa, and even my excellent collaborator, would use *pīli* in translating Prof. Bergson's fine passage on the intellectual joy of creative effort and attainment. Once we get at the psychologically composite backbone of *pīti:* "intellectual excitement over an object felt as desirable,"[20] we may render the word by whichever of the abovc-named terms—none of which, not even 'joy,' is bare feeling—the particular context seems to demand.

This mood of intellectual commotion, ranging from interest, eagerness, or zest up to rapture, is too important in all religious psychology for us to dismiss the Buddhist discussion of it for yet a few moments longer. The emotion, writes the Commentator, reaches maturity and climax in composure and serenity of mind. But the prior working of it is a sort of mental intoxication. We may pass over his metaphors of the first three and the last: the 'goose-flesh' thrill, the lightning flash, the boiling surge on the shore, the expansion of a blown bladder.[21] It is on *pīti* as elation, or transport or ecstasy, that he enlarges. And here he quits our Western and Greek-trained sobriety, and takes the elation[22] and transport physically as well as mentally, representing those possessed of this rapture "caught up to the third heaven," as St. Paul might say, "whether in the body or out of the body I cannot tell—God knoweth," or as he himself says, "making the body elated, so as to accomplish a measure of leaping into the air." He then tells two anecdotes from his abundant store: how an Elder M. dwelling at N. contemplating the full moon at a shrine, and thinking how at the Great Shrine all the faithful must just then be reverencing the Buddha, dwelt on the idea of Him, and in a throbbing *(ubbega)* ecstasy, like the chords of a lyre, rose in the air and stood again in the courtyard of the Great Shrine. Thus too the daughter of well-to-do folk at Y., near the minster Z., left at home while they went to church, stands at her door looking in the bright moonlight up towards the hill-shrine 'shining like a heap of pearls,' and longing to hear 'the sweet Dhamma-discourse.' Thereupon throbbing ecstasy arises and she too leaps into the air, arriving in the congregation before her parents. They question her and are amazed that she should have come as only arahants were wont to travel.

Pīti therefore at this degree of intensity was held to have produced, in the past at least, a similar supernormal result to the power of supernormal will,[23] without apparently any express preparation or exertion of will.

Buddhaghosa gives his cases in much the same tone of habituatl, unsurprised faith that an orthodox Christian would use in alluding to miracles. But. I have not yet found him attesting his own experience of such results, nor that of his contemporaries. And his chapter on Iddhi in the *Visuddhi-Mogga,* to which he here and there refers his readers, is to me clearly not that of one who spoke from first-hand experience. When this chapter appears in its long-delayed English dress, the reader will be able to judge to what extent the Jhāna exercises, prescribed for making the mind *(chitta)* 'concentrated, purified, pliant and fit,' seem calculated to induce the extraordinary power of will which, in the *iddhi*-adept, were reckoned able to convert mind into body, or body into mind, as if the repudiated Ātman itself were immanent in either.

The work of Buddhaghosa cannot, let it be once more said, be justly appraised in these fragmentary remarks, typical of the very unfinished state of our 'excavations.' His intellect, clogged as it is by all that usually handicaps the scholastic mind, dominates the development of his own tradition: unsound philology, unsoundness as to historical evidence, the losing, in detailed work, all conspectus of the whole, whether that whole be the movement of thought in his day, or the movement, from its inception, of the tradition he represented. His diction, moreover, becomes at times involved and ambiguous. He was no longer writing for a culture with no literature. But there is a world of difference between his commentatorial phraseology and the limpid periods of Milinda's delightful monitor.

We know, however, enough to be doubtful as to the probability of coming upon any attempt to theorize on the problem of representative cognition, or of the association of ideas. Apparently he resembled in this respect European philosophers prior to Hume and Hartley—for Spinoza's statements[24] carry us no further than Buddhaghosa's as psychological theory, though they are better summaries. Until, in fact, the *neurological inquiries* of Cartesianism were set on foot, no strong impetus arose to make the apparent parallelism between the physically associated and the mentally associated a matter for philosophy to theorize about. But the problem of the functions of the pineal gland and the deductions therefrom set the savants thinking new. "I wonder," wrote Spinoza, "that one who had so often taken to task the Scholastics for wishing to explain obscurities through occult qualities, could maintain a hypothesis, beside which occult qualities are commonplace! What does he understand, I ask, by the union of the mind and the body?"[25]

Now Buddhist psychology postulated a seat, literally, site *(vatthu)*, for each of the ways in which the organism was, as Prof. Bergson might say, canalized for access to external impressions, or rather for the access of those external conditions, in consequence of which *chitta* or consciousness was called up. These were the five special sense-peripheries, and, in the older books, "that material thing on the basis of which apprehension and comprehension take place,"[26] a thing which, in all the (much later) commentaries, is explained to be the heart *(hădăyă-vatthu)*. The brain is not even mentioned until the *Milinda,*[27] and though the etymological parallel of nerves *(nahāru)* is always included, in the enumeration of the thirty-two main constituents of the body, it is apparently in the sense of 'sinews.' There was therefore no physiological induction concerning th 'canalization' of sensory disturbance. Hence any corresponding theory of 'latent mental modifications,' based on a theory of neural tracks and so forth, is no more to be expected in Buddhist than in European mediaeval psychology. And so far as I have seen, Buddhaghosa is content to push no further the adumbrations of theory we met with in the *Milinda,* but simply to give the facts, the results of representative cognition, without feeling called upon to frame any new theory to suit the 'non-entity-non-soul' axiom of his tradition which he loses no opportunity of upholding.[28]

To judge, however, by S.Z. Aung's able presentment, in his introductory essay to the *Compendium of Philosophy,* the later mediaeval and modern psychological literature of Burma and Ceylon has not only evolved a detailed theory of reproductive mental procedure, but claims to have evolved it from the so-called Method of Relations, formulated with interminable detail in the last book of the Abhidhamma-Piṭaka called *Paṭṭhāna.* We have as yet no access to the original documents containing these later developments to which Mr. Aung owes his philosophical training. But I imagine that it will have been the contact with Western thought and criticism, and not his authorities, who prompted him to propound and to reply to the query: "How is memory possible, if the subject be not the same for any two consecutive moments in life?"[29]

There is a prospect, I am glad to say, of a fuller disquisition on Buddhist philosophy of mind, on the lines of Mr. Aung's essay, by his teacher, Ledi Sadaw, coming our way. I have put in a plea that special attention may be given to the philosophy of relations *(pacchăyă),* and its application to mental processes.[30] Here is not the place to discuss it, and the question itself given above is philosophical, and not psychological. We are not, however, out for psychology pure and simple, and shall do well to pause a moment over the subject on which we may get more light in the near future.

Pacchaya is not exactly our relation. It is nearer to that kind of relation which we call *causal.* Thus, in the Commentary on the Book of Relations Buddhaghosa writes: "*Pacchaya* here means *because-of-that-makes to-go.*" (This is the media-eval 'buried-city' etymology common to Europe and Asia.) "That is to say, it is concerned with what is *not-opposed.*" (More 'buried-city.') "For the phenomenon *(A)* which stands or happens in non-opposition to another phenomenon *(B)* is said to be the *pacchaya* of the latter." We now become more positive again: "*Pacchaya* has the essential mark of *rendering service* (literally working-up-to, *upakāraka). A* is *B*'s *pacchaya* in so far as it renders service to *B*'s existing or becoming. *Pacchaya,* condition, reason-why, source, coming-to-be, origin *(pabhăva),* etc., are one in meaning, different in verbal form." Judging by this passage, therefore, the twenty-four kinds of *pacchaya* distinguished in the Book of Relations are twenty-four ways in which the happening of *A affects* the happening of *B;* or conversely, in which the happening of *B* is as it is because of the happening of *A.*

When this definition is applied to the correlation of one mental moment *(chitta)* with another, we get a much less empty abstract conception than that of two terms just 'standing in relation one to the other.' We come to realize that in a continuum of momentary *chitta*'s we have *not* just a number of isolated, mutually independent units, simulating by their speed a unity of substance, just as a red-hot point whirled round in the dark simulates an unbroken circle.[31] We *have* a number of units simulating unity, but they are such that each one is what it is because of the 'service-rendering' of those that have preceded it. Thus according to the Book of Relations, and the echo of it in the *Compendium,*[32] *B chitta,* related to *A chitta* as (1) immediately succeeding, (2) present while *A* is absent, (3) present with *A* in abeyance, that is, telling upon it, is, in consequence, so and not otherwise. Or again when *A* and *B* are in the *pacchaya* of association *(sampayutta), A* has rendered such service to *B* that it is wrought up into *B,* and hence in *B* our past appears as present. (In the latter case reference is not made to mutually contiguous *chitta's.).*

This influence, or service-rendering, or conditioning of one momentary phenomenon (whether mental or otherwise) came to be termed *satti* (Sansk. *śakti),* that is ability, *vis,* influence, force, chiefly, it would seem, through the teaching of Ariyavaṃsa, a notable and noble-natured Burmese teacher of the fifteenth century.[33] And I mention the theory as showing that the Buddhist theory of non-soul, or of no abiding entity which-*has-chitta*'s, has not caused the sub-stitution, in place of such a doctrine, of disconnected momentary monads, each one being a *tabula rasa* of anything that had gone before.

All this is insufficient to explain the 'reinstatement' of any given section of the past at any given moment, in other words, why *chitta*'s *A B . . . call up* certain former *chitta*'s *X Y. . .*, whether we add, with Locke, why *C* is the consciousness that 'we did have' *X Y . . .* once, or whether we do not. But that is a matter that the hypothesis of a perduring entity does not explain either. Theories of association may state that, for instance, a man, passing some object one day and making a remark, may recollect, when passing a year later, what he said, and continue the conversation, and call it association by contiguity and similarity. But the *form* of persistence, the actual mechanism of reinstatement, that has gone on 'in' the mental continuum, the theory can no more describe than the electrician can say how wire or ether is molecularly affected during transmission of electric force. We cannot describe mental experience, which is 'much more vast than cerebral life,'[34] in terms of space, nor can we broaden into detail in terms of time.

Hence the sublimated animism of a 'psychic continuum' is really no better off as to an intelligible description of memory than is the Buddhist non-animism. If the former seem at first sight to help us out, it is because we have been surreptitiously conceiving mind in spatial dimensions, either as a storehouse,[35] and modified substance, or else as a long, long lane down which come pilgrims from the past. Such at least is, I think, the vaguely floating image of the remembering mind held, if not by psychologists, at least by the general reader. If we strip off these quasi-visible vestments of mind, and think of it only in terms of its processes experienced as results, then the upspringing of potential *chitta*'s, not empty and mutually disconnected, but each fraught with the informing *satti* of this or that among former *chitta-continua,* brings all our past right up to and about our present at least as much as does a real, and not a simulated unity in the *continuum.*

In putting down the *Compendium,* we note that, in the last part, which is concerned with that mental training, or 'making to become,' so as to realize, for those who were ripening for it, the final goal of life, the word *paññā* has gone, and *vipassanā,* dis-cernment, insight, has replaced it. The twin terms, 'calm and insight,' date from the oldest books, but they come, as twin terms, to the very front rank only in mediaeval works. Each now comprises a *khandha* or group of exercises. 'Calm' *(sam'ăthă)* includes all that Buddhaghosa classed under *samādhi* (concentration) and the older books partly under training *(sikkhā)* of *chitta,* partly under *pañña.* Under 'calm' is now included 'supernormal intellection,' or *abhiññā.*[36] Of its six modes the last—the spiritual 'destruction of the *āsava*'s or vicious instincts'—is suppressed, and the other five are very briefly dismissed. 'Insight' comprises the intellectual realization of certain truths.

In spite of the ample statement given to one of them, to *iddhi,* in Mr. Aung's interesting introduction, I see in these altered proportions an evolution of thought. Sixteen hundred years, perhaps, had elapsed since the wonderful age that produced the Founder and his Arahants, and over a thousand, since the earliest records were committed to writing. Even Buddhaghosa could only refer to the marvels achieved by saints of old, while it would seem that for Anuruddha's still later age, the sight and sound of things ineffable, and the godlike will that could say of Brahma-heaven "Be thou near to me!"[37] were become as things that were very far away.

Let me bring to a close these fragmentary inquiries into the age-long career of Theravāda thought by linking those into the *chitta* and the *paññā* of the oldest books with the latest utterances from Burma. In the Thera Ledi Sadaw of Mandalay are combined, fortunately for us, a desire to give of his best to those in Europe who have ears to hear, and a culture that is quite untouched by anything that Europe might have to give him of its own thought. His diction, so far as I know it, seems to me ageless; his similes might all be in the Nikāyas, or in Buddhaghosa; his ideas belong to a machine-less world. Such a product must, even in Burmese monasteries, be soon a thing of the past. Fortunately his works, written in Pali, are numerous, and are in print. In them (I do not say in them only) we may learn something of modern Theravāda, undistorted by filtration through minds born and trained in European tradition. Such 'distortion' may eventually bring about an evolution in Theravāda greater than any it has experienced—an evolution that will eventually react mightily on our own philosophic standpoints—and be ultimately acknowledged by Buddhists themselves as the cause of a great renascence. For the present we need to record this uncontaminated, unleavened heritage, deriving without break, from the Burmo-Singhalese Council of AD 1165, not to mention the cult of the preceding centuries.

"*Chitta* (consciousness), *mano* (mind), *mānasa* (intelligence), *viññāṇa* (awareness)," writes Ledi Sadaw, "all are really one in meaning: they are various modes of coming to know.[38]

. . . *We know,* whether our knowing be of blue as such or not as such, or whether it be of 'the real, as real or as otherwise, or whether it be what we desire or do not desire. Now knowing is three-fold: there is knowing as being aware of, knowing as perceiving, knowing as understanding. Perceiving is a clearer knowing than awareness, and is also knowing without forgetting over a lapse of time. Understanding *(pajānana)* is knowing adequately by way of class and species. It is knowing completely all about any [given] knowable thing. For even in anyone such thing there is much to be known, *viz.* as to its nature, conditions, correlations, effects, the evil, the good of it, its impermanence, the ill connected with it. And *pajānana, paññā,* is to have an exhaustive knowledge of all this, as it is said: 'The limit of knowledge is the knowable, the knowable is the limit of knowledge.' *Paññā* in its fullest sense is omniscience. . . . Yet even for the learner, whenever through coming to know he conquers natural failings, his knowing has become *paññā*. . . And whenever ordinary folk by coming to know dispel what is harmful, induce what is good, their knowledge too is *paññā*."[39]

The writer refers to passages in the canonical scriptures illustrating each kind of knowledge. A little further on he launches into a disquisition, varied by dialectic, on *chitta* as "the especial basis, the peculiar soil of the error of Permanence," and on the doctrine of *chitta* as a phenomenon "which uprises and ceases from one moment to another." From the standpoint of popular thought and diction, it is correct to speak of mind, person, soul, as being or persisting, or passing hence, when from the standpoint of ultimate or philosophical truth nothing of the kind is so. We will not go into that here. But we can pick up the thread again for a moment, where his discussion is psychological.

"Knowledge *(ñāṇa)*,[40] do you say, is the criterion of truth? But that knowledge is twofold: inferential or intuitive.[41] When ordinary folk are investigating abstruse, subtle, deep matters, they know by way of inference. But with proper mental training, by developing *paññā,* they may attain intuition in such matters. By intuition, they discard the concepts 'person,' 'entity,' 'self or soul,' 'living thing' *(jīva)*, and know things as of purely phenomenal nature, under the concept of element *(dhātu)*. Now mind, mental coefficients, matter, Nibbāna,[42] are just such abstruse, subtle, deep matters, to be truly understood only as inferential knowing becomes, through persistent training, transformed into intuitive knowing."

Here we see intuition considered as one aspect of that *paññā,* which is thorough knowing.

It may be noticed that Dr. Ledi makes no reference to Buddhaghosa's frequently repeated simile of the child, the citizen, and the gold-expert (above, pp. 131 f.), when distinguishing between the three modes of coming-to-know. Mr. Aung tells me that it is given in Sumangala's still more popular commentary. He himself disapproves of consciousness *(viññāṇa*) being graded with perception and *paññā,* which belong to the philosophically different category of mental coefficients *(chetasika*'s).

Here the reader of the Nikāyas and Buddhaghosa will note that the ancient five-group distinction is passed over. Ledi Sadaw, however, in commenting on that classification, has illustrated, by a new and ingenious parable, the functions of the five 'groups,' in vindication of the adequacy of this ancient category to take into account all human activities in such spheres as are governed by natural desire *(taṇhā-visayesu ṭhānesu)*:[43]

"It may be asked: Why did the Exalted Buddha, when classifying conditioned experience under the concept of aggregates *(khandhā)*, make the number five? We reply: By these five groups of phenomena our acts, regarded as felicific, on occasions where natural desires have play, find accomplishment. This the following parable may illustrate: A wealthy man, seeking wealth, builds a ship, and equips it with a crew of fifty-two sailors. By transport of passengers he amasses money. Of the crew one is expert in all works relating to the ship, and has these carried out; and one is acquainted with the ports to be visited and the routes thither, and he from a commanding position[44] directs the steering. The owner, maintaining boat and crew, receives and enjoys the ensuing wealth.

"Now by the sea we may understand the way of life ever renewed *(saṃsāra);* by the ship-owner, a person pursuing natural and worldly desires. By the ship we may understand the material aggregate *(rūpa-kkhandha);* by the wealth it brings in, the aggregate of feeling; by the former officer, the aggregate of perception; by the crew carrying out his orders, the mental properties labelled as *sankhāra*-aggregate; and by the latter officer, ho directs the ship's course, the *viññāṇa*-aggregate.

"'Feeling' covers all our enjoying, partaking of 'Perception' includes our conversance with, our intelligence of, our competence respecting all experience in the range of things human, divine, or infra-human. That which we call *sankhāra*'s covers all that we do by thought, word, or deed according to what we have perceived. And *viññāṇa,* or the aggregate of consciousnesses or cognitions, is all those sense-impressions, sense-cognitions, which act as heralds and guides wherever we happen to be, pointing out, as it were, in our daily activities, and saying: 'this is here, that is there!' Thus it is that the five aggregates cover all that is wrought within the range of natural and worldly desires."

Hence, in this our little inquiry over some twenty-three centuries or more, we are still, in these words of last year, well within sight of our starting-point. In them we see that, with a considerable evolution in introspective and analytical and critical power, there has been and still is an unbroken current of consistently upheld Theravāda tradition, and that, even for a writer credited with so much independent and progressive judgment as Ledi Sadaw, the word ascribed in the Piṭakas to the Buddha, adored and omniscient, delivering his first sermon, in the Deer Wood near Benares, has not yet passed away, nay, has not, since that auspicious day, lost aught of its pregnant and far-seeing wisdom and power.

References

1. *Compendium,* 284.
2. I do not say that we do not meet with this division in, and its acceptance by, Buddhaghosa. My point refers only to emphasis.
3. See above, p. 89.
4. *Compendium,* p. 198, cp. 213; cp. above, p. 23.
5. *Visuddhi-Magga,* ch. xiv.
6. *Visuddhi-Magga,* ch. xiv.
7. Above, p. 174.
8. *Compendium,* 126.
9. P. 69.
10. *Atthasālinī, 73; Bud. Psy. Ethics, 2, n. 3.*
11. *Atthasālinī,* 263, Note the orthodox scholastic mode of definition.
12. *Atthasālinī,* 309.
13. *Ibid.,* 108f.
14. Printed as yet only in Burmese characters, this work is now being prepared for publication in Roman letter by the Pali Text Society.
15. *Atthasālinī,* 317.
16. *De Anima,* II. vi.
17. *Atthasālinī,* 311.
18. *Bud. Psy. Ethics,* § 9.
19. *Atthasālinī,* 115.
20. Discussed in my *Buddhism* (1912), p. 231.
21. *Visuddhi-Magga,* ch. iv.
22. *Udagya = ud ag- ya* (up-top-ness).
23. *Adhiṭṭhānā-iddhi,* see pp. 127f.
24. *Ethics,* II. xvii, xviii.
25. *Ethics,* v. Preface. He is referring to Descartes.
26. *Compendium,* 278.
27. *Questions,* i. 42.
28. *Bud. Psy. Ethics,* xxxvi f.
29. *Compendium,* 42.
30. *Paṭṭhāna,* part II., was edited by myself in 1906; part I. and the Commentary I am now preparing for press.
31. Cp. *Compendium,* p. 33, *n.* 1.
32. Page 193, § 9.
33. Cp. Mrs. Bode's *Pali Literature of Burma,* 41. I owe the information to S.Z. Aung's kind reply to my question as to the earliest mention of *pacchaya-satti.*
34. Prof. Bergson, 'Presidential Address,' S.P.R., translated by Dr. Wildon Carr.
35. A *boîte à souvenirs,* Prof. Bergsoj would say.
36. *Compendium,* p. 209, and above, pp. 126–30.

37. *Visuddhiagga. 'Iddhividhā.'*
38. So Buddhaghosa.
39. *Yamaka,* ii., Appendix, p. 264 (P.T.S. ed.).
40. Ibid. 274. This to the objector.
41. *Paṭivedha,* lit. penetrating.
42. The fourfold category of Buddhadatta and the *Compendium.* See above, pp. 174–76.
43. I have very slightly condensed the following.
44. I felt tht 'the bridge' was too modern for this 'ageless' prose!

Bibliography

AUTHORITIES

The Four Nikāyas (or 'Bodies' of Doctrine): *Dīgha, Majjhima, Saṃyutta, Aṅguttara.*

The Fifth Nikāya.

Miscellaneous books.

These five form the Sutta-Piṭaka. The quotations are from volume and page of the Pali Text Society editions.

The Abhidhamma-Piṭaka.

Seven miscellaneous books.

The above, together with the Vinaya-Piṭaka, form the Canon of Theravāda scriptures. The Four Nikāyas (to mention no more) are all pre-Asokan (Asoka's probable date is BC 272–235.) The only portion of such as are quoted which are translated into *English* are:

(1) *Dīgha-Nikāya,* I, II—*Dialogues of the Buddha,* I, II, in 'Sacred Books of the Buddhists.' The remaining volume is in preparation; to be continued by *Majjhima-Nikāya.* See also *Buddhist Suttas,* 'Sacred Books of the East,' vol. xi.

(2) *Aṅguttara-Nikāya,* Parts I, III By E.R.J. GOONERATNE. Galle, Ceylon, 1913.

(3) *Dhammapada* and *Sutta-Nipāta,* 'Sacred Books of the East,' xi, and other translations.

Iti-vuttaka (Sayings of Buddha). By J. MOORE, 1908.

Psalms of the Brethren and Sisters. By Mrs. RHYS DAVIDS, 1909, 1913. Pali Text Society.

The Jātaka. Cambridge, 1895–1907. These are from the Fifth Nikāya.

(4) *Dhamma-sangaṇi (Buddhist Psychological Ethics)*. By Mrs. RHYS DAVIDS. Royal Asiatic Society, 1900. This is in the Abhidhamma-Piṭaka.

Buddhism in Translations By H. WARREN, 1896, gives excerpts of different dates.

TRANSLATIONS OF LATER WORKS

The Questions of King Milinda. By T. W. RHYS DAVIDS. 'Sacred Books of the East,' 2 vols.

The Compendium of Philosophy. By S.Z. AUNG, B.A., and Mrs. RHYS DAVIDS. Pali Text Society, 1910.

Thoughts on Buddhist Doctrine. By LEDI SADAW, translated by Mrs. RHYS DAVIDS. 'Journal of the Pali Text Society,' 1913–14. Also H. WARREN, *op. cii.*

The mediaeval texts referred to, but not translated, are given in the footnotes.

Index

Supplementary Chapters

10

The Buddhist Principle of Change[1]

There is a view of the general fact of change which all philosophies would endorse and confirm. This is the popular view, inimitably expressed by the French proverb: *Tout lasse, tout casse, tout passe.* It is also, with corollaries, the religious view. "The life of man passes by like a galloping horse, changing at every turn, at every hour" (Chwang-tzu):

"Change and decay in all around I see.
O Thou who changest not, abide with me!"

Albeit it is worth mention, in passing, that in all world-religions the emphasis thrown on the great fact of change is curiously slight save for the notable exception of Buddhism. Exponents of this creed have not failed to bring out the insistence they have found on change as thus envisaged.

But philosophy, once it gets astride of this 'galloping horse' of change, may go further than either the popular or the religious view. It may say: ultimately, fundamentally, there is only change. Repose, fixity, permanence, are illusions. There are in reality, *i.e.* beneath our customary way of perceiving, no immobile thin s that get moved externally, or that persist in time, breaking up gradually. They are fictions of sense and intellect. "Thengs are changes, but no things that change."[2]

Buddhism, like Christendom, stands not only for a popular and for a religious culture of many branches, but also for a philosophy with a history. Where, in respect of such a philosophical gallop, does Buddhist philosophy get up and ride, and where does it dismount? Does the attitude of Theravāda doctrine (I mean, of the philosophic thought evolving for many centuries, first in Northern India, then in Ceylon and Further India) correspond at all in its nature and its range to, say, that notable outcome in European philosophy which we associate at present chiefly with the name of Henri Bergson?

Is it reasonable to try to trace any degree of correspondence, of parallelism, of resemblance? Some say it is not. M. Henri Bergson, on the other hand, was good enough to admit to me that he was struck by such a correspondence. And that is a worthy passport to a further word on the subject. There is no question here of present dynamic concepts having evolved from these particular concepts of a past and now barren era of thought. The connection—if connection there be—is just this: Given certain conditions in the growth of a local nucleus of human ideas, these ideas will take a certain line. If this be admitted, we may look for, we may expect to find, this line followed by more than one local nucleus so conditioned. That many circumstances of time and space may differ in the one nucleus of travailing minds and in the other will not prevent the minds from following that line. But they will profoundly modify it. In this way history does and does not repeat itself.

In the modern nucleus we have, on the one hand, a philosophic departure which has, at the back of it, a development in the sciences of matter of some centuries in duration. And we have some centuries of *literary* philosophizing.

In the older nucleus, we find a much earlier philosophical evolution which has, at the back of it, a very scanty development in the sciences of matter and a very limited tradition of a philosophizing *with the pen* (or stylus). And, further, the documents of this evolution are as yet, to a mere European, most imperfectly accessible. In knowledge of them we have scarcely got beyond the corresponding position of Christian culture at the beginning of the Renascence, which knew little of its Plato, and had its Aristotle largely fron Arabian sources, and which was scarcely aware of its own poverty in materials. So even now Indologists, pursuing the Theravāda philosophy no further than the Commentaries of the fifth century AD, discuss the submergence, in India, of Buddhist metaphysic in the rising flood of Vedāntism and other mediaeval-lines of thought, oblivious of the quietly continuous development that appears in the works of Buddhadatta, Anuruddha, Sumangala-Mahāsāmī, Ariyavaṃsa, as well as of Dr. Ledi Mahāthera of present-day fame—to mention no others—who have handed on the torch of psychology and philosophy in Ceylon and Burma. Until, however, by the quietly persistent work of the Pali Text Society, editions, not to mention translations, of the typical writings of these luminaries are produced, it is a difficult matter for even a reader of Pali to acquire an historic perspective of Theravāda philosophy in its continuity. My excuse for speaking on it at this immature stage is that we have at least a little more than the foot wherefrom to speculate about Hercules.

And whereas the obstacles I have named are an historic fact that can in nowise be got over, so that Buddhist philosophy, even up to the present day, will seem archaic beside the scientifically and linguistically finished products of European thought, there is, in comparing them *as philosophies of change,* always this interesting feature to recollect: The philosophic tradition of Europe, rejecting the Herakleitean theory of change as more real than fixity, suffered the written expression of it to die, and its influence to be handed on chiefly in the scientific speculations of the Atomists. In its turn, and after many centuries, science has imposed a philosophy of change on Europe. But Buddhism literally built its philosophic foundations on a theory of change. With the whole field of science in a relatively rudimentary state, it grasped by intuition a principle of change which, in many features, anticipates that which we have seen put forward to-day as the result of profound investigation and analysis.

Here there will be no further word on those conditions impelled by which the nucleus of Theravāda philosophizing followed a line suggestive, at least, of the line followed by the modern philosophy of change. This is not a sketch of Buddhist philosophy. It is only a straying into a field from which Buddhist psychologizing was never fenced off. Those conditions should be sought in the history of philosophy ancient and modern.

What then is that principle of change as grasped by Buddhism? Let us examine its earliest expression in the oldest Pali books. Here anyway the evidence is entirely accessible. There are still obstacles to a complete understanding, as I shall presently indicate, but at all events the Pali Text Society has published all the oldest materials.

The fact of universal and continuous change is expressed by several more or less synonymous terms: *a-niccha,* impermanence; *añña . . . añña* (=the Latin *alter. . . alter),* 'now one, now another'; *aññathatta,* otherwiseness, alteration; *vipariṇāma,* fluctuation; *khaya,* dissolution ; *vaya,* evanescence; *vāya,* mobility; *bhava,* becoming; *udayabbăya,* rise and evanescence, and others. But the first three are employed in the passages most crucial for our purpose.[3] In fact they exhaust the two shades of meaning in our own curious, if useful, Latin term 'change.' Take anything you like that is obviously changing in time or space, material or mental, *x*—at any given moment *x is,* at another moment *x is not.* Thus *x* is impermanent, 'in the sense of not being,'[4] as the Commentators say. Or *x* is now *x* with a coefficient of *y,* or if you like of *n.* Thus *x* is altered *(aññathatta),* and may proceed to alter so much that eventually we call it not *x* but *y.* At a given moment a baby boy lies on my lap. At another given moment a young soldier leaves me for the war. My baby is gone, changed; my boy has evanesced.

In the older books of 'Suttas'—the Four Nikāyas—change is usually presented in this latter guise of the evanescent or impermanent, fleeting, transient. The other notion of 'other wiseness' is used in more analytical Suttas of a psychological or philosophical content. The reason is fairly obvious. The Buddhist movement, as we know, was at the outset a movement of protest, dissent, reform in matters religious, social, ethical. It saw its chief enemy in the current and popular beliefs as to certain things being permanent, eternal, a ground for a feeling of rest and security in belief—of ill-based rest, of false security. Namely, in the great mystery of life there were believed to be these three stable, real, perduring things: The I or soul of man; the world wherein that soul was born and could be reborn; the life in heaven once attained, The doctrines of the Dhamma or cosmic law denied permanence to all these things, It took for its ultimate view a vitalistic aspect of things. That is, it saw everything *sub specie vitoe,* as being governed by the law of life. What is that? To be subject to birth and to decay and death, with an apparent, more or less static interval between. As we might generalize: life might be renewed in recurring geneses, but it could not persist eternally in any conceivable phase, else it was not life. Buddhists did not so generalize. They did not speak of 'life' as we do. They spoke of becoming *(werden),* of birth and death, of 'going on' *(saṃsāra).*

Thus the physical world considered under each of its main constituents: earth, water, fire, air—resolved in all Buddhist philosophy to these four elements: the extended, the cohesive, the calorific, the mobile—and as composing either human bodies, or other substances, is said 'to manifest evanescence, to dissolve, to be subject to impermanence, transience, to perish.'[5] And this verdict is extended to the universe as a whole, which periodically undergoes involution and evolution *(saṃvaṭṭa, vivaṭṭa).*[6]

Again as to life in heaven, Suttas on legends concerning the celestial spheres and their denizens relate of complacency felt by gods[3] in the security of their tenure: "This our life is permanent *(nicca),* fixed *(dhuva),* eternal *(sassiăla),* absolute *(kevăla);* influctuate in its nature; without rebirth, decay or death; and beyond it is no further salvation." Then the

Buddha, intuitively knowing of this delusion, transports himself to that world, and on being greeted with a display of the same confidence, shakes, as it were, head and finger at them: " Alas! the good god! how ignorant he is! Alas!. the good god! how ignorant he is! inasmuch as he will be calling permanent, fixed, eternal, absolute, bound to persist, that which is impermanent, mutable, temporary, relative, and bound to end. . . beyond which there is a different salvation."[8]

Lastly as to the soul or spiritual principle in man—I have elsewhere pointed out that the Buddhist argument against such a permanent entity was levelled not against the belief in a changing, growing soul, that could yet, unlike all other mental or physical phenomena, defy death, but against the belief in an *unchanging divine* soul that transmigrated, as the soul in other cults is held to do. The argument runs that nothing supremely divine, *i.e.* perfect happiness, power, and immutability, can be claimed for a human being who, as essentially changing, must inevitably, sooner or later, suffer and suffer helplessly.[9]

Next as to the use of the philosophical terms 'otherwiseness,' 'becoming otherwise,' 'alteration.' In one of the many analytical discourses on organ and field of sense we read: " Because of two things sense-impressions arise, namely because of a given organ and a suitable object. Now each of these two is always impermanent and changing and having a state of otherwiseness. Thus the dual process itself is vibrating and fleeting and evanescent and changing. Its conditions are so; how should the impression itself be permanent? And the feeling and the perception arising in consequence, these also are necessarily vibrating and fleeting, evanescent, changing."[10]

Once more, to take a concise philosophical statement: "All conditioned things[11] have three characteristics. They arise, they evanesce and they have otherwiseness of duration."[12] Thus the static interval, if it be more than a limiting point, is only apparently static. It too is changing. And the relatively swift and all-inclusive 'becoming-other-ness' in mental life is brought out in a curious simile. "Nothing in the world equals the rapidity of *chitta* (consciousness, mind).[13] It is hard to find an illustration to show how swiftly mind comes and goes." "It were better if the unlearned man in the street considered this body of four material elements as the soul of him rather than mind. Wherefore? The body may last anyway for years, even a century or longer. But what is called mind or intelligence or consciousness, arising and ceasing in the night, is other than that which arises and ceases in the day. It is even as a monkey in the forest, travelling through the timber, clutches one bough, looses that and clutches another."[14]

The curt wording in the archaic Sutta is felt by the Commentator, Buddhaghōsha, to be ambiguous, and he guards the reader from inferring that any day or night-long duration of a conscious state was here intended—a heresy refuted elsewhere in the Canon.[15] For, he adds, in one instant many myriads of 'consciousnesses' arise and evanesce.[16] This elaboration in explicitness of the apparently more leisurely rate of change as illustrated in the Sutta came about during the 1,000 years or so that elapsed between the compiling of the text and Buddhaghōsha's new edition of the Commentary.[17] And later Commentators screwed up the rate of mind-flux even higher.[18]

The earlier documents, as we have seen, bring us thus far, that of the two elements in the notion 'change,' namely impermanence and alteration, nothing whatever in this conditioned universe is permanent. Everything, but especially mind, is perpetually altering, as composite phenomenon, nay even in its elements, and is either coming to be or passing away or undergoing intermediate change. The ancient canonical phrase *sabbe sankhārā aniccā*—"all things are evanescent"—has ever been and is for the Buddhist a motto parallel to the *kismet* of the Muslim. And the surviving work on his doctrines next in point of time after the Canon and nearest to it in sanctity—the *Questions of King Milinda*—is in this matter equally emphatic: "There are three things, sire, which you cannot find in the world. And what are the three? That which, whether conscious or unconscious, is not subject to decay and death—that you will not find. That quality of anything which is not impermanent—that you will not find. And in the ultimate sense there is no cognition of a personal entity."[19]

Let it not, be supposed that this decided attitude is characteristic of Indian literature generally. There is no such emphasis to be found in any of it that is pronounced to be pre-Buddhistic. The only occurrence of the word 'impermanent' in any but late Upanishads is in one verse of the *Kaṭha Upanishad,*[20] itself not among the oldest; and even this is declared by Dr. Deussen to be a later interpolation, so much is it in conflict with the context.

Besides this emphasis on universal change, the Suttas give us the notion of change as an orderly or determined continuity. The series of phenomena that interested most deeply the early Buddhists, as they interested Sokrates a little later, were those of life, especially the vital phenomenon of mind. And it is to life and to mind that we find, in the Suttas, the first application of those two figures so closely associated with the dynamic speculations of Herakleitus—the stream and the flame.[21] They became in later Buddhist thought no less closely bound up with its central principles. But this is not true of it at its inception. For all the wealth of simile and parable in the Suttas, and the Anthologies of the Fifth Nikāya, and in spite of the fact that no simile occurs oftener than 'river' and 'fire' *(nădī, aggi),* they are for the most part used to illustrate other doctrines than that of impermanence.[22] The way of the good life, the Magga, is also compared to a stream *(sôta),* and he who has embarked upon it, the 'convert,' is called *sôtāpanna.* The long way of one's lives is also called the stream of becoming (*bhava-sōta*).[23] And the conscious continuum is once called *viññāṇa-sôta.*[24] The kinetic being of fire is once called in to illustrate: "my perception was as the flame in a fire of chips, changing as it rose and ceased."[25] I think this is all. But in the little eleventh-century manual by Anuruddha, *Compendium of Philosophy,* the *vade mecum* to this day of the Buddhist student, the *sota* stands out in its terse and dry paragraphs: "So... consciousness *(citta)* . . . after rebirth goes on, in the absence of any process of cognition,[26] in unbroken flux like the stream of a river till the uprising of death-consciousness."[27]

I cannot as yet quote a mediaeval application of the flame simile. But here is flame used as a striking instance in the latest words of Buddhist philosophy, written, after all these centuries, especially for the English reader: "Just as that flowing river or burning flame appears to those who contemplate it as a mode of motion, not as something static, and the motion itself consists in a continuous process of vanishing past acts and of manifested fresh acts, so all these determinations into various, 'acts' are only series of distinct phenomena, mental and bodily, made manifest by way of arising and ceasing."[28]

But putting similes aside, we have, I repeat, to see that, even in the older books, the notion of change was conceived, not as successions of fortuitous discrete happenings, but as orderly, connected processes. The Buddha is represented as confronted with two extreme views. One is that of the Permanent Self: *A* does the deed; *A* reaps the result, *i.e.* in subsequent happiness or unhappiness. The other is that of the Absolutely Different Self: .*A* does the deed; he ceases to be. *B* reaps the result. Was either view right? No, the Buddha replies; there is a middle doctrine which is right; and he repeats the formula known as Arising by Way of a Cause.[29] Perhaps we feel baffled and have recourse to the Commentary. There we read: "Here he shows that there is neither a doer nor a feeler in any ultimate sense, but that any effect *[lit.* fruit] comes from its conditions, and that without the conditions comes no effect." And far better than this is the same Commentator's explanation in another cognate context: "If we understand the effect or fruit as something arising in a series, we get no absolute identity or diversity, so that we cannot say the result proceeds from the same, or from something quite different. So we look in the adult for the results of something we cultivated in the child."[3]

We may regret that the Buddha did not, according to his editors, expound his Middle Way more as, for example, a Bergson would now discuss it. But twenty-four centuries stretch between the two prophets. Moreover, whereas the French seer can record in peerless phrase his own views, Gotama taught his orally, and these were only perpetuated in writing after inferior minds had for centuries handed on his half-forgotten, half-understood pioneer ideas. The Buddha was perhaps the first Indian thinker to state causation as a universal law valid for mental as for physical life. And his standpoint, that a person so called was just a stage in, and a label for, a causal process among composite phenomena, was for his hearers striking and pregnant, far-reaching in its effect. It led subsequent thinker to envisage the universe of changing phenomena and constituents of phenomena under the aspect of an orderly causation proceeding by way of *upakāra,* or 'assisting agency.'[31] That is to say, *X* in causing *Y* was conceived as assisting Y to become, and that by being passed on into, or wrought up into, *Y* And thus anythingis *what* it is, *as* it is, not fortuitously, but as a 'fruit' or result of an antecedent thing. Yet a little later in time the *upakāra* notion of a fecundating cause is developed into that of *satti (= śakti),* a term old as the Vedas, connoting (like Carlyle's 'canning') ability, efficacy, force. Ariyavaṃsa, for instance, an eminent writer of Burma in the fifteenth century, speaks of the *pacchăyasatti,* the causal force.[32]

The Greeks began to think in terms of force good deal later than the Buddha's day. Aristotle uses the word 'by force' *(βία)*[33] but makes no fruitful use of it. Pali had also, of course, words to the same effect—*sahasā, pasayha*—but it did not occur to the early thinkers to apply either these or *satti* to philosophical theories. It was not till Stoic thinkers developed Aristotle's theory of causation, exploiting his adumbrated 'active' and 'passive'—*τπὸιοûυ, τὸ πασχον*—that the antithesis of force and matter started on its career as the corner-stone in European cosmology: the pusher and the pushed. The relatively late appearance in Buddhist philosophy of a term equiva]ent to *vis* is an interesting problem. To answer it, we might derive a suggestion by first discovering why, in the third century BC., the Mediterranean thinkers developed the science of physics. The Stoic philosophers of Cyprus, the Aegean, Italy, Carthage were contemporaries of Archimedes. In connection with what other knowledge did the term *śakti* influence mediaeval Buddhists?

Gotama Buddha may have been, relatively to his *milieu,* a master of knowledge *(sabbaññu).* But if there was, for him to take up and utilize for his teaching, no body of positive scientific knowledge, it follows that there would be no words of pregnant import for him to use. It is not historical honesty to read into the archaic diction of the old Suttas more than the knowledge of their times could fairly be said to express. On the other hand, the longer one studies them, the clearer seems to be the want, for an intellect far above the level of its age, of tools—tools in the shape of scientific materials, concepts, terms. We seem to feel the mind of 'the immcasurablc Gotama'[34] labouring under this want in its pioneer questing. He could scarcely appeal to his hearers' intelligence, in expounding a theory of a self-fecundating flux in terms of force or influence, lest they should see in those terms a reference to the personal intervention of a theodicy or divine fiat—a notion which was precisely what all his teaching left on one side. Personal intervention is the sense in which *βία* 'by force,' appears in the *De Animā.* If, as M. Ed. Le Roy writes, "the function of philosophy is to criticize the works of knowledge,"[35] then must philosophy wait upon knowledge, that is upon the growth of science.

So much is clear from the Sutta: in the evolution of the act,[36] not on and the same person persisted as self-identical, sowing and reaping, nor were sower and reaper totally different. The latter was a causal outcome of the former. Or, as Buddhist philosophy preferred to say, the reaping was a causal outcome of the sowing. Later developments came to see in the process, by the aid of developed knowledge and new terms, phases in a continuous series of force-wrought changes, changes which meant that each imagined unit in the series was assisting agent to the next, by passing over into it, informing it, wrought up in it. But to the Buddha's hearers, the only explanation that would mean anything more or less intelligible would be a reference to the newly formulated doctrine of cause and effect. This theory was set out in abstract terms, to this effect, "that "a cause is that without which an effect cannot come to be." It was also applied to the ever-recurring life of a sentient creature in terms of sentience, viz. as suffering *(dukkha*).[1] The latter form is usually employed, and by the Theravāda tradition to this day has been regarded as stating, no less than the abstract formula, albeit in less general terms, a doctrine of universal causation. As claiming to solve the problem of apparently persistent personal identity in a cosmos of unceasing change, it is of the greatest interest in our inquiry. It is the expression of the theory of becoming ascribed by his Church to the founder.

This is borne out by its employment in another Sutta to reconcile two metaphysical extremist views: "All is;" "Nothing is"—so similar to the Greek antithesis as represented by, say, Melissus and Gorgias.[36] The elements of matter and mind are for Buddhists ultimate realities. But they have never associated permanence with these. They are 'conditioned,' 'produced by causes;' they arise and cease; they are perpetually becoming

Leaving these pioneer intuitions, let us notice a few points in the mediaeval explications of them bearing upon our inquiry.

First with respect to the elements of matter. Matter or *rūpa*—a word almost as broad in import as 'phenomenon'—is defined as "that which changes its form under the physical conditions of heat, cold, etc.," following the older definition in the Suttas.[39] And the four essentials or elements in any material phenomenon, however relatively concrete their meaning may have been in the older books, have come in later philosophy to signify extended quality, cohesive quality, calorific quality, mobile quality. Every material phenomenon is compact of these four in differing proportions. Hence the whole material universe has this element of mobility, 'vibrating or oscillating; moving its co-existent qualities from place to place.'[40] And since, in addition to this conception of essential movement, there is the yet more fundamental property in it of becoming and evanescence, since, moreoyer, there is no concept of inherent rest or rigidity to counterbalance in space or time this mobility, but only relatively static intervals in which change (otherwiseness) is still proceeding,[41] we may fairly say that in the Buddhist physical world movement is more 'original' than rest.

With respect to mind this has been already made out. In the original books the notion of a constant mental continuum, interrupted by fully conscious processes of perception, etc., is not, as far as I can discover, clearly made out. Such processes are said to arise from external stimuli and to constitute something which, in becoming, was not previously in existence. "Have I not taught thee by many methods that consciousness arises from a cause; that except from a cause there is no coming into being of consciousness? . . . Do ye see, bhikkhus, that it is something that has become *(bhūaṃ);* that the becoming is according to the stimulus; that if the stimulus cease, then that which has become ceases?"[42] The notion of some sort of mental life, however, ever proceeding as a concomitant condition or factor of life itself, soon emerges, in the latest book *(Paṭṭhāna)* of the Canon, in the term *bhavanga*—'factor' or 'condition of becoming,' 'becoming' standing for existence or life. Coming to the *Milinda,*[43] we find it compared to the flow of life in dreamless sleep. And in the citation above from the *Compendium* it is compared to a river, and is *contrasted* with mental life when intellectual processes are going on.

Here we come to a very striking anticipation of modern theory. I have used the phrase 'interrupted' by conscious process as characteristic of the Bergsonian hypothesis. In fact, it was a sentence in Dr. Wildon Carr's *Philosophy of Change* that lit up for me the significance of the Buddhist language: "Elements of experience. . . are. . . interruptions of movement. . . ."[44] Interruption involves arrest; and our intelligence, building itself by the lessons of touch-based vision, is held (in the Bergsonian hypothesis) to create a world of fictitious static 'states' and 'things.'[45] If it were built up by the teaching of the ear, the world as we know it might wear a very different aspect.

But M. Bergson is, unwittingly, more Buddhist than Dr. Carr, for he uses the actual Buddhist term of cutting on or into. "Things are constituted by the instantaneous cut which the understanding practises, at a given moment, on a flux of this kind."[46] The *Compendium of Philosophy* states the traditional theory of perception thus: "When, say, a visible object. . . enters the avenue of sight and, the life-continuum *(bhavanga)* vibrating twice, the stream of that continuum is cut off, then consciousness. . . of an apprehended visible object arises and ceases." Thereafter, according to the relative intensity of the stimulus, follow the remaining moments in a full act of perception. And "after that comes subsidence into the life-continuum."[47]

There exists quite a group of later Commentaries on this manual, but I am not yet in a position to state that anyone of them is prepared to see that the act of perception, thus conceived, implies a principle of change as the fundamental reality.[48] The manual itself seems to be concerned simply with the (very concise) exposition of currently accepted doctrines in the interest of students, even to the extent of doggerel mnemonic verses as summaries to each section, and to be putting forward no fresh developments requiring discussion. Nowhere, indeed, have I yet met with any Buddhist disquisition conscious of the temerity we may feel in consenting to, let alone putting forward, a theory that our intelligence, trained for racial life by sight and by the need for action, subjectively arrests the 'flux of reality,' creating fictitious 'states,' like the arm of a London policeman in the mid-stream of traffic. For us this late-born temerity—this revenge of rejected Herakleitus—may be a back-wash of the wonderful passing of sixteenth-century astronomy, revealing the daily lie told us by our senses of a static earth, of a sun as mobile adjunct. It may have required a Copernicus to breed a Bergson.

But Buddhist philosophy may be said to set out with the position that its proper function is the inversion of common (*i.e.* popular, conventional) sense; that the opinion of the man in the street (*puthujjăna,* many-folk) is never more than conventionally right; that the true, the real, is not the apparent.[49] Hence it saw, perhaps, no need to defend the gradual and *natural* evolution of its own original, never rejected doctrine of impermanence and 'otherwiseness.'

It is a natural step from sense-perception to memory. The Bergsonian theory of change has revealed to Europe that a philosophy of change, when conceived *sub specie vitoe,* can put forward a sounder explanation of memory than any theory of a persistent modifiable self, however much such a theory might purge itself of popular spatial notions, such as the *boīte à souvcnirs,* or a sort of bagatelle-score memory, with pegs moved along a line of life. The living continuum has its past wrought up into itself, recalling to the imagination George Eliot's pretty phrase: "As the sunshine of past mornings is wrought up in the bloom of the apricot." Our problem is not how we remember, but how we come to forget. Remembering becomes negative. The problem becomes this: the elimination of what we would forget.[50]

Now while the Buddhist theory of cause as assisting agency, and as an informing influence *(satti),* coupled with a full and interesting theory of relations, into which I cannot enter here,[51] enabled the philosopher to explain memory after a dynamic fashion, I will here only mention that Pali literature has no specialized term for memory, from its beginning till the present day. *Sati* (Ssk. *smṛti),* as pointed out above, "is not wholly covered by 'memory,' " it is "rather the requisite condition for efficient remembrance or thought of any kind, namely lucidity and alertness of consciousness. It is a quality rather than a specific *direction* of consciousness," expressing the opposite of distraction and of superficial thinking.[52] The more perfected your *sati,* the better can you penetrate present realities, review the facts that are past, foresee the events that are coming.[53] Buddhist mental training might be called one long insistence on the need of *sati.*

If it be asked whether Buddhism conceived the flux of things, whether material or mental, as essentially indivisible and only 'cut' into states or units, or as successions of momentary units, discretes, or particulars,[54] I am not yet prepared to give a documentary reply of an adequately historical kind. I could give instances of mind referred to as minds or 'consciousnesses' ('*chittāni'*) of momentary duration, but very few. The rule is to speak of *chitta* in the singular, of *dhammā,* which may mean mental things or 'states,' in the plural. But to judge by the writings of Mr. Shwe Zan Aung,[55] present Buddhist philosophy insists strenuously on the essential unity of this mental life as a flux in time. "Each 'one-momentary' state of consciousness *(eka-kkhanika-cittuppādo)* is logically complex, but psychologically of a single indivisible whole." He uses the Bergsonian simile of the spectrum.[56] And he applies the 'assisting agency' definition of cause in expounding this unity. I cannot trace a similar insistence in the case of physical change and movements in space. Nor have I yet elicited from him any traditional authority equally explicit on the subject. But he refers to the *Compendium* as expressing indivisibility in any given mental complex. This is not quite the same thing as indivisibility in duration of a series of so-called states.

To turn for a moment to the field of commentarial legend: it is not irrelevant to notice how, in certain stories, religious conversion is brought about through the power of the Buddha being exercised to accelerate the normal rate of change in the life-flux. Some youth of either sex, much obsessed by physical beauty, is made to see the vision of a lovely maiden swiftly maturing, ageing and falling crumpled up on the ground. And the much-shaken beholder is recorded in one case, as saying :

> "*As bidden by some power age o'er her fails;*
> *Her shape is now another, yet the same.*
> *So this myself, who ne'er have left myself,*
> *Seems other than the self I recollect.*"[57]

Such a vision modern applied science could no less give us, were someone to be photographed with sufficient frequency during a lifetime in one pose, and were the films then cinematographed with that rapidity so much affected by the cinema mechanic. As applied to the life-history of plants, the method is impressive. Will Christian teaching ever unwittingly plagiarize Buddhist legend by securing the life-reel of some persistently devoted human specimen?

This fragmentary and inadequate statement of the scope and significance in the Buddhist principle of change must here end. Further materials, as has been said, may enable a more complete essay on the subjcct to be compiled. But it may be said by those who are acquainted only with Buddhism as a religious movement of the sixth century BC that we cannot expect to find in its doctrine any disinterested philosophical theory; for is not Buddhism, first and last, the study of an Ideal, of a Goal, of a Way Out, of a Danger and an Escape? Would not any doctrine of change as the great reality in life be studied, not disinterestedly, as a problem in the quest of truth but chiefly in relation and subordination to the Great Escape, namely from pain and sorrow and the causes thereof?

There is truth here as far as the statement will carry us, but it does not take us all the way. There is a parallel in Christianity. That started as a Gospel of Escape, and ended by becoming established *as* European culture, and annexing all the secular learning of those centuries during which it was sole director of all the schools. In the same way there is a considerable difference in urgency between the missionary Suttas and the works written long after the establishment of the *Sāsana* or Order as paramount and its annexation, first of Indian culture, then of the philosophic intelligence in the countries it converted.

Nevertheless there is a unity in the evolution of Theravāda thought that cannot be claimed for that of Christian philosophy, with its pagan annexations. That being so, we might well look to find the Theravāda ideal borne on the stream of universal flux, like the Most High riding upon the wings of the storm.[58] We find the contrary. It will not see in Change a star—to take Emerson's metaphor—to which it might hitch its wagon. It was so occupied with the fatal certainty in life, that happiness was bound to evanesce and change into unhappiness, that it forgot the other swing of the pendulum, that the blissful sense of returning happiness was *also change.* Life and experience were said to be painful, or liable to pain, *precisely because they were ever changing.* And life and experience, in Buddhist tradition, had been going on for each person a most awfully long time, no man knew how long. The completed perfected person had surmounted all change, save a few years of the last of his lives. *Anicca* is ever a term of baneful import. Even the blessed and beneficent changes as the aspirant passed into stage after stage of the path of assurance, and broke fetter after fetter—even these are never labelled as modes of benign *anicca* and otherwiseness. And the final release from life after the saint's death though never discussed, is alluded to in terms of non-change as the unborn, the unageing, the undying, the permanent, the uncaused. Nirvāṇa is held to be the one and only state that is both desirable and permanent: "Eternal like Nibbāna."[59] The saint was held to have had enough of—

"*Spinning down the ringing grooves of change,*"

and gladly said:

"*Well! of all that now have I made an end!*"[60]

And I find nothing to correspond to the eternal youth that pulses in Bergson's sentence: "The more we steep ourselves in the sense of universal becoming, the closer we feel drawn to the principle in which we live and move and have our being, an eternity of which must not be an eternity of immutability, but an eternity of life and of movement."[61]

And yet—. More than one writer has called Buddhism the gospel of a senile decadent epoch in the history of India. Yet it is noteworthy that, in the whole of Pali literature, one goal is never invoked as desirable, and that is Rest. The Arahant is said to have laid low his burden, to have done his task, but concerning that task the words for tired, weary, and rest simply do not occur.[62] Greek philosophy hovered around the notion of rest; Christian hymnology welcomes it; the modern Hindu poet tells us somewhere: "The waves of turmoil are on the surface, and the sea of tranquillity is fathomless."[63] Buddhist philosophy and anthology both regard as supremely desirable energy, concentration, insight, serenity. And far away for most, near only to but a few at any time, there is held to be the one 'state' of utter peace,[64] inconceivable in content and undescribable, since concepts and speech are the children of *life.*[65] It is a curious paradox. Or if my feeble torch throws its ray amiss, it may kindle a clearer light from elsewhere and—

"Ita res accendent lumina rebus."[66]

References

1. This and the following chapter were published in *The Quest* (London, October, 1917), and are reproduced here, with emendations, by kind permission of the editor, G.R.S. Mead.
2. H. Bergson, *La Perception du Changement* (Oxford, 1911), p. 24.
3. Dr. Ledi distinguishes, under *a-niccha,* metastasis (*vipariṇāma)* and subsequent modification (*aññathādhāva). Vipassanādīpanī* (Rangoon), translated by U. Nyana. *Vāya* is *primarily* 'wind,' *Udayabbaya* = udaya *v(y)aya.*
4. *Abhāvaṭṭhenāti aniccaṃ.*
5. *Majjhima,* i. 185 f.
6. *Aṅguttara,* ii. 142; iv. 100 f.
7. *I.e.* by beings who have lived as men on earth.
8. *Saṃyutta,* i. 142. Cf. my *Buddhism,* 1912, pp. 58f.
9. Cp., *e.g. Majjhima,* i 138; *Vinaya Texts,* S.B.E., i. 100.

10. *Saṃyutta,* iv. 67 f.
11. *I.e.* all things that have arisen through a cause (*sankhăta*).
12. *Aṅguttara,* i. 152.
13. *Aṅguttara,* i. 10.
14. *Saṃyutta,* ii. 95.
15. *Points of Controversy,* p. 363 (*Kathāvatthu,* xxii. 8).
16. *Sāratthappakāsinī,* the Commentary on *Saṃyutta.*
17. Based on older versions.
18. Cp. *Compendium of Philosophy* (P.T.S., 1910), p. 26.
19. S.B.E. edition, ii. 102. On thelast sentence cp. *Points of Controversy* (P.T.S.), p. 8.
20. II. 10.

    "A thing I know, a treasure, transient.
    How win from transience the influctuate?
    Therefore I built the Nāchiketas-fire,
    And won thro' transient things th'influctuate."

    Quite possibly a reverberant Buddhist influence.
21. He 'flourished' 80 years later than, *or* almost coincidently with, the Buddha, according as we use Buddhist *or* European dates for the latter.
22. Cp. my 'Index to Similes in the Nikāyas,' *J.P.T.S.,* 1906–7, 1908. Dr. Oldenberg (*Buddha,* 6th ed., 1914, p. 299) maintains the opposite with regard to fire; and Mr. Dhalke sees in the Buddha's Fire Sermon a cryptic meaning of the *Inkraft* (inner force) of karma (*Buddhismus als Weltanschauung,* 1912, pp. 54f.). But the contet, taken with other fire-allusions, points only to an analogy with fever, inflammation, and the writers do not convince me.
23. *Saṃyutta,* iv. 128.
24. *Dīgha,* iii, 105.
25. *Aṅguttara,* v. 9.
26. See below, p. 234.
27. *Op. cit.,* p. 153.
28. Dr. Ledi, 'Some Points in Buddhist Doctrine,' *J.P.T.S.,* 1913–14, p.159. Cp. also *ib,* p.146, the Herakelitean use of flowing water and permanent 'river' by one who has certes never read of Herakleitus, unless it were through a Burmese book.
29. *Saṃyutta,* ii. 20.
30. *Visuddhi Magga,* ch. xvii.
31. Commentary on the *Paṭṭhāna.*
32. Not Lucretius's simple apposition *vis causaque,* but *cauoe vis. De Rerum,* i.
33. *De Animām* iii.
34. *Thereagāthā,* 1089.
35. *A New Philosophy* (London, 1913), p. 144.
36. *Kamma-vivaṭṭa,* a term ascribed in the same work (*Saṃyutta,* i. 85) to

the Buddha :
"*Thus* by the evolution of the deed,
A man who spoils is spoiled in his turn."

37. *Ency. Religion and Ethics,* art. *'Paṭicca-samuppāda.'*
38. *Saṃyutta,* ii. 17.
39. *Ibid.*, iii. 86; *Compendium,* p. 271.
40. Ledi Sayadaw, *Paramattha-dīpanī* (Rangoon), p. 240.
41. See above, p. 222.
42. *Majjhima,* Sutta 38.
43. ii. 163.
44. *Op. cit.* p. 39.
45. *Creative Evolution,* p. 261.
46. *Ibid,* p. 262, *'la coupe instantanée.'* Cp. also pp. 331.
47. *Op. cit.*, p. 125 f.
48. A transcript of the most modern of them has just arrived from Burma, and I hope that a transcript of the most classic among them is in preparation.
49. Cp. *Points of Countroversy,* (P.T.S., 1915), p. 63, *n. 2; Buddhist Review,* 'Expositions' by Ledi Sayadaw, 1915, pp. 253 f.; *J.P.T.S.*, 1913–14, 'Some Points of Buddhist Doctrine, p. 129.
50. Cf. with this the usual attitude to past consciousness of Matthew Arnold's lines:
"Ech day brings its petty dust
Our soon-choked souls to fill,
And we forget because we must,
And not becauso wo will."
51. S.Z. Aung in *Compendium,* p. 42; *J.P.T.S.*, 1915–16, Dr. Ledi, 'On the Philosophy of Relations.'
52. See above, p. 90.
53. Cp. Bertrand Russell, *Our Knowledge of the External World,* p. 234.
54. *Ibid.*, p. 150; and *The Monist* (1915), p. 405; "The real man too, I believe, . . . is really a series of momentary men, each different one from the other, and bound together . . . . by contnuity and certain intrinsic causal laws."
55. *E.g.* 'The Philosophy of the Real,' *Journ, Burma Research Society,* April, 1917, p. 8.
56. *Introduction to Metaphysics,* p. 11.
57. *Psalms of the Brethern,* cxviii.; cp. *Sisters,* p. 82.
58. *Pss.* xvii. 10; vix. 3; *Nahum,* i. 3.
59. Sassato hoti Nibbānena samasamo. *Kathāvatthu,* p. 34.
60. *Psalms of the Sisters,* p. 163.
61. *La Perception du Changement,* p. 37. Or this : "Humanity . . . is one immense army galloping beside and before and behind each of us in an overwhelming charge able to beat down . . . . the most formidable obstacles, perhaps even death" (*Cr. Evol.*, p. 286.

62. Save perhaps for two lines in the Sister's Anthology, by a weary housewife and an old lady respectively, ver. 1, 16. It is also true that, in the Sutta on rebirth, quoted below, p. 247 f, rebirth as man, as deva, and the winning of the final goal, are all likened to happiness after a toilsome, perilous journey, albeit the world 'rest' does not occur.
63. Tagore.
64. Santipadaṃ. Santi is peace, calm, not rest.
65. *Sutta Nipāla,* 1076, '*Whereby one might speak of him,* that for him is not."
66. *De Rerum,* 1115.

11

The Buddhist Doctrine of Rebirth

This is in outline what I have to say: Buddhism gave the world a more definite doctrine, cult, or theory of rebirth than any other religion or philosophy before or since. From our present point of view, sharpened by a few centuries of scientific inquiry, it is indefinite, unfinished, a patchwork, and by the rather one-sided emphasis of aftermen somewhat obscured and strained.

In the original doctrine, so far as we can really get back to it, we find:

(1) The fact of rebirth accepted as universal law ;
(2) The whence and whither of rebirth fairly well defined;
(3) The acceptance of rebirth of the whole self, both mind and body, not of discarnate mind or soul;
(4) No very positive information as to the 'how' of rebirth.

The naïve simplicity of the doctrine as to the 'how' is obscured: *(a)* by an unfortunate ambiguity of language at a place and a time *(b)* by a certain mystic theory involving that ambiguity, and attacked by early Buddhism only; *(c)* by the well-meant efforts of the Fathers of the Buddhist Church to expand the logic of certain tenets; *(d)* by our own imperfect knowledge confusing later with early doctrine; and *(e)* by the materialistic taint in our own psychology.

1. In the early literature of India it is not till we come to the Suttas of the four Pali Nikāyas that we find the vague earlier belief in life after and life before this life on earth gathered up in anything approaching a definite orderly

doctrine. In the Vedic hymns any indefinitely long survival of life is a matter to be prayed for, the gift of gods or of 'fathers.' In the Brāhmaṇas and early Upanishads there are various modes of pre-existence and survival asserted. The former assertions are much on a footing with similar ones by Empedokles. In the Upanishads there is no consensus of belief. Leaving aside on this occasion the teaching of the Jains, it is only in the Buddhist Suttas that we find aspirations and speculative assertions reduced to the acceptance of a certain scheme of pre-existence and post-existence as a law of nature. You were and you will be, whether you pray and sacrifice, or whether you do not. Your life is taken up into the causal law of the universe. And this was a new standpoint.

How was it expressed in words?

Special terms for this continuity of life here or there are far more to seek in the Buddhist books than in our own discussions on them. Rebirth, reincarnation, transmigration, survival, metempsychosis—all are Western labels. Terms that we do find are the following:

(1) Recollection by some saintly person of how and where he or she lived in many 'lives' prior to this is called. recollection of former 'residings ' *(pubbenivesânussati)*.

(2) Different spheres of existence are called 'the three becomings' *(bhavā)*.

(3) The Buddha is asked as to the destiny of certain individuals who have recently passed away.

(4) Worldly desire leads to 'again-becoming' . . . he "at the death of the body is on his way to a body."

(5) The Buddha calls the whole business, past, present, and future, as a long, long 'faring on,' a 'running on,' of you and of me.

(6) The most usual term, perhaps, is just 'fappening' or 'arising' (*uppajjati*), after 'falling' or 'deceasing' *(cuti, cavati)*. There is no spatial emphasis, in these terms, of going up or down as in the Christian legend of the Ascension. The term descent (*avakkanti*) is applied to consciounsess finding a new home in some sort of body. But if children were born,

like Athēnē, from the parent's head, it is quite possible that the current term might have been 'acent.' We are concerned in this chapter with pre-scientific language.

Many more allusions to individual pre-existence and individual survival might be quoted; enough to show it as a very important assumption or datum in Buddhist doctrines, namely that a man in deceasing lives on; that he has so deceased and lived on times without number; that the beginning of his life is not revealed; that the end of it, that is, of the deceasings and rebirths—not of being itself—*is* revealed. Nowhere is this datum evded. No query is raised when the Buddha claims pre-existence under nother name : "I was then that Brahmin chaplain . . . I was then the young Jotipāla. . . . I was then that wheelwright." It has become an old and popular tradition. It was taken up into the doctrine of karma, *i.e.* of the power of the will and its outcome in action to shape the doer's destiny. "Lord!" babbles the crazy Ophelia, "we know what we are, we know not what we shall be." "We only know," said the Buddhist standpoint, "what we are when we know what we have been and what we may be."

2. The possible whence and whither also were in this doctrine brounght into clearer relief than before. "Five goings (or bournes, *gati's*) are there," the Founder teaches: *nirăyă,* that is hell or purgatory; the animal kingdom; the realm of the *peta's* (or *manes*); the earth-life of men; the deva-worlds. "Each of these I know, and the way to each. And there is Nibbāna; that I know and the way to it" (*Majjhima,* i. 73)

This is the simplest, possible the oldest, Buddhist category. The fifth *gati* was in its contents not so simple. It was, so to speak, a dumping-ground for not only survivals in eschatologial beliefs, but also for the imagination of the Indian mind playing about with its four logical alternatives; A is B; A is not B; A is both B and not B; A is neither B nor not B. Thus rebirth as a deva may be of body only; it may be of mind (the incorporeal) only; it may be of both body and mind; it might be of neither. And so a place is found for beings living a mindless life, and for beings living an incorporeal life—both of them unimaginable by us, as yet. And they are, as we might expect, as lifeless as logical abstractions would be. The mindless devas only live, for us, when they begin to think, whereupon they promptly die (*Dialogues of the Buddha,* i. 41)! And the bodiless devas are practically only fetches of abstract thinking, without life or light or love. Where we are shown any inmates of the four unseen *gati's,* we find creatures of both body and mind analogous to ourselves.

3. That this was the relatively simple unsophisticated belief in the earlier days of the Buddhist age—in so far as Suttas and the tradition handed down in commentarial stories faihfully reproduce this—may be seen in the alleged cases of intercommunication between the three last named of the five worlds. In the case of the Peta's—a form of rebirth that may well be Buddhism's annexation of the then decadent survival among the common folk of the once-powerful Fathers-cult of the Vedas—we find communication was possible between such beings and humans who were psychically developed—clairvoyants and clairaudients, as was Great Moggallāna, one of the two chief apostles of Gotama. He, the stories tell, could and did see and interview these Peta's, ill-born because of misdeeds in their past earth-life. They are reported as dwelling round the walls of the earth-villages in (invisible) dwellings sometimes highly decorated. Sometimes they are rocorded as comely, but all, always or intermittently, are suffering some more or less appalling penalty in the *body* because of their ill-deeds; and their term of suffering could be shortened by the transferred merit of their human kinsmen's benevolent acts. Thus they are to each other as substantial in body as earth-people are to each other, and have average intelligence. Their world was the centre of their universe, and if they looked longingly for help from earth, it ws analogous to our looking for help, uplift, and consolation from a world 'above,' which is not as

substantial a conception to us as is our own world.

But—and here is where the Buddhist mind is interesting—their world was not 'above' nor 'below.' It was right here, interpenetrating our own space. This is a more significant concept for us than it used to be. It was easy for Christian belief to rest in an 'up into' heaven' (Luke xxiv. 51) and a 'descended into hell' when space had not been charted by astronomy as far as thought can reach, and there were no Antipodes. But we do not now believe in a survival on the moon or stars or, with the Veda hymns, at the back of the sun. We have to learn to conceive not so much, not so wholly, an otherwhereness as an otherwiseness. One day this will constitute the great, the most practical problem in Relativity for us. It may be that, in a space that is one for all worlds, the otherwhereness may be inward, and, for the rest and more than that, it may be just 'otherwise.'

Between 'devas' and men intercommunication is not infrequently met with in the Suttas. The deva-worlds are in a way remoter than the peta-worlds—it is a much later book that gives an attempt at a measured *descent* from one of them[1]—but the idea that you have to ascend into either the more earth-like kama-devas' world or the less earth-like rupa-devas' (or Brahmas') world is not made apparent. To visit either from another world was possible only to the saintly who were psychically developed, or to a deva. The transit is effected by an effort of will analogous to that put forth in a vigorous voluntary gesture "Just as a strong man stretches out his flexed arm, or flexes his outstretched arm, so X vanished thence and appeared in Y," the world in question. All the preposterous, if decorative, symbolism of wings is in this literature undreamt of. "Seated cross-legged, he can travel through air as a bird on the wing," is the nearest approach to it.

And once in those bright realms *(svarga* or *sagga)*, the earthly visitor does not find himself among 'discarnate spirits'—a very impossible conception for us, as yet—he is with men and women apparently as complete in body and mind as himself. They see him, walk to meet him, take his arm, and talk—all, of course, impossible without bodily organs. So when devas come to earth they use arms and legs and voice and wear clothes (*e.g. Dialogues,* ii. 37). They were longer-lived, more mobile, happier than earth-folk, and had the power of reading thought. Such were they in their deva-conditions, but *in kind* they were human men and women. Of the earth they had been, of the earth many of them would be again. As it were clothes, they have changed bodies, and therewith the psycho-physical reactions, but they are not bodiless.

You will note that I speak of 'devas,' and not, as the word is usually translated, 'gods.' It is true that the denotation of 'god' is wide and diverse, but the word should not be strained. When is a god not a god?

A god is a god when he has, if not perhaps creative power, at least informing influence, controlling force, some sort of cult and votaries, some power to bestow or withhold, aid or harm, reward or punish. When he has nothing of all this, at least outside his own sphere of life then he is no god. In the Vedic pantheon we do get deities having these attributes. But in the later age, when Gotama formed his *sāsana* or Church, it is only Brahmins who are still worshippers of survivors in that pantheon; it is only the common folk who have their little local cults of this or that *devatā.* The devas who now and then pay or receive visits, on earth, at home, are nothing more than so many ladies and gentlemen, pleasant, courteous, respectful to great earth-teachers or earnest disciples. They have, it is true, their governors, but these too are not immortal, but have been, and will probably again be, denizens of earth.

No, Buddhist devas are not gods. And one way to understand Buddhist doctrine is to cease calling them so. It is curious that while Christendom has always maintained its constant, if very vaguely conceived, doctrine of survival, it has never coined a good word for the survivors. But it has been hampered by its want of light as to the body in which 'we' survive, and by its myths of a waiting sleep and of opening tombs. Pure spirit is as yet an impossible conception. When progress in the theory of survival becomes more generally intelligent, either a word for 'survivors' will be found, or we must hold by 'souls'—souls that we *are,* not souls that we *have.* For that word is capable of covering both mind and body, as in the wireless call S.O.S. (save our *souls!*).

4. What did the early Buddhists hold happened at rebirth? In what did rebirth consist?

This seems to many inquirers to be a dreadful *crux.* And, indeed, must it not always be so when, on the one hand, we are dealing with, if not a primitive, yet with a prescientific attitude of thought, and when, on the other, we do not ourselves know the relation between 'ourselves' and our bodies?

Yet may it not be that, to a certain extent, we have created more of a puzzle than there should be? And by 'we' I include writers on Buddhism, old and new. In fact, it is they largely who are to blame. It seems curious, but it is a fact that, whenever these writers get explicit on *how* Buddhism conceived rebirth, he, or she—I too have sinned!—always goes, not to the old Suttas, but to the later books. But the Founder taught for years and years. And there was no Paraclete descending after him to teach his followers. What is wrong with the old Suttas ?

What happened, according to them, when a man or woman came to die? They did not say there would be at once rebirth on earth, for they said this was improbable. They classed, speaking generally, the other four bournes under two heads: the unhappy 'downfall' to either Niraya, Petas, or animals, and the happy coming-to-be in deva-world.

There was yet a third eventuality—that of the final Nibbāna or Parinibbāna of the perfectly 'Worthy' (arahā), the Saint. He by his perfect saintliness eluded all five *gati's* or goings, for he ceased to 'go on,' *i.e.* to be once more reborn and to die. Somewhere, somehow, he passed into a rest from going on. That he had ceased to exist it was not right to hold

(*Majjhima,* i. 140). That he had a mere respite from rebirth was unorthodox (*Points cif Controversy,* 212). But for the race to whom Gotama's mission came, as there was no new revelation of the Alpha of all things, so there was none either of the Omega of all things. It does not, of course, follow that there was no Alpha or Omega because none was revealed through him. But just there and just then man was to try to go alone through a rather dark valley. And few were fit for Arahantship.

For everyone else it was rebirth, on the one hand, as nerayika, peta, or animal; on the other, as man, as a kāma-deva or as a brahma-deva, according as, by an unexplained automatic sequence, his voluntary acts had been predetermining destiny. In passing it is, perhaps, worth commenting on the absence, in all the wealth of simile, parable, and symbol, in the Piṭakas, of those scales of doom so familiar in medireval Christian thought. Yet weighing, of thing and thought, figures in Indian literature.[2]

Well, the man when his term here is up—to use the refrain: 'at the separation of the body[3] after death'—finds himself 'arisen' in a new world with a new body. 'Himself?' I hear the readers, of books about Buddhism ask. That is so. For all practical purposes, as we say—'conventionally understood,' as later Buddhist documents say—when some Ānanda dies, it is Ānan a who 'goes on.' It may not be an identical Ānanda's self, but that is because Ānanda's self is ever changing. It is not quite a different Ānanda, for it is the beginning of, say, chapter 500,001 in the life-history of this individual now called Ānanda. But it is much more the 'same old' Ānanda than ever you or I could be. And he will very likely keep his name. Thus we read of the rich patron of Gotama's Order, Anāthapiṇḍika, revisiting the Jeta Grove at Sāvatthī—his gift to the Order—from the next deva-world[4] and being seen and heard psychically by Gotama and Ananda, and recognized *as* Anāthapṇḍika. And, to name only one other such episode, we read of Gotama telling his disciples how the Licchăvi soldier Ajita, who had recently died, had appeared to him to denounce a certain would-be rival fakir as a liar. "He has been telling people I am reborn in purgatory. But I have become a deva in the world of the thirty-three [the 'nearest' deva-world]."[5] The Buddha does not say 'the man who was Ajita. He speaks of him as 'Ajita the Licchăvi general.' The essential individuality, therefore, is considered as unbroken.

No doubt in the case of rebirth as an animal, name and human mentality are the one wholly, the other largely, lost. But outside folk-lore and the garrulous Commentaries, no actual cases of a rebirth as animal recognized by a teacher's supernormal insight have I as yet met with. The Buddha is made to affirm in a few Suttas *(e.g. Majjhima,* iii. 167) that some classes of wrong-doers will meet with such a fate, but the Suttas, so far as I know, contain no other special illustrations of it.

But in this kind of rebirth and in that of earth-humanity, while the entrance of the self or person finds no adequate treatment, the acquisition of the new body is a relatively simple matter. Parents of some sort were ever making new bodies, but it is quite maintainable that no parents, animal or human, ever made new minds or new selves.

If we next ask whence came, in Buddhist belief, the new body, when a man passed on to appear as inmate of purgatory, as peta, or as deva, there is not a word in the teaching about it. In each case it is evident that there was a new body, and that is all there is to say about it. Nor were the founders asked concerning this—so far as the records show. The age was in such matters not critical. Ready to their hand, had they thought it either true or a teaching expedient to adopt, was the notion of the finer body set free from the tissues of the earth-body during the deep sleep of the latter. For it is not a 'discarnate spirit' that then comes forth from the earth-body, but the man's self invested in a finer vehicle, leaving only the breathing life to guard its 'nest.' By this bright light-body he 'looks down' at his sleeping members, and "goes again to his home, golden person, lonely bird," has a pleasant time of sport and laughter and love, or sees fearsome things, learns things good and evil, and hastens back, when the earth-body is waking, to dissolve into it again like rain or vapour. And thus the dream at waking is a memory, not of strange, unaccountable earth-fancies, but of the adventures during sleep, albeit distorted by a flicker of earth-memories. The Upanishad dealing with this belief is reckoned usually among those that are pre-Buddhistic *(Bṛhadāraṇyaka).*

Psychology is occupying itself much with dream-consciousness. Is it possible that Indian psychologists may one day look into their ancient lore and find it, as well as the present, in the phrase of Leibniz, *'gros de l'avenir'* ? But early Buddhism took up from the outset a position of manifold protest against current theories. And it may well be that one of these (to which we are coming) barred the way against its accepting light from the teaching we find in those earlier Upanishads. The theory of the subtler body as our self's new home at death would have sufficed to explain—hypothetically, as we should say—all bodily rebirth not of parents. But it is left untouched. We have even, in one of the Suttas, a description of the symptoms of death in a deva[6] (and of his friends' valediction as his return to earth draws nigh), but nothing about the arrival of a worthy man among devas.

But what about the rebirth of a new mind? Is it a brand-new mind that is reborn? Is the doctrine here also unfinished? We are now dealing in a way with four-fifths of the earth-person; for of his corporeal and incorporeal constituents, the corporeal occupies but one *khandha* or aggregate, the incorporeal aggregates are four in number, and all are what we call mental. What has the Buddha to say about a new mind at rebirth?

Nothing. Mind is a perpetually changing movement of arising and ceasing *(Saṃyutta,* ii. 95) : this is said generally, not concerning a new life-spell. As he might have said: "It is no fit question."[7] If he had lived now, he might well say, it is as if, when a man takes down a worn-out electric battery and sets up a new one, he were to ask, Why have you sold me no new electricity? The electric force would be potentially ready all the time, though unable to work without the battery and the bell-push. All we need, at dying, is a new battery. *We* are the force; our translation into this is mind.

But you will say that is how a modern Buddha might express it, who had learnt to think in terms of forces. How did the Buddha express it?

This is a very fit question. He was, introducing more analytic care into his teaching than had been done previously, but he could not draw parallels from a stock of knowledge that was as yet non-existent. So he spoke of mind *(viññāṇa)* getting a new station, standing, platform *(ṭhiti),* in a new body. This did not mean that mind, for him, was itself a stationary thing, as if it was a head fitted on to a bust. He saw not mind, but minding; not consciousness, but a 'consciencing,' analogous to an act of handling. We handle pen, typewriter, diary. When these are done for, we renew them, but we do not buy new handling of them. Thus at death there was a *bheda,* a separation of the body, from that 'mind,' by which word we express the self, but the dying was of the body only. We need not be misled by the little parable of the' burden-bearer.' *(Saṃyutta* [iii], xxii. 22, 1). There the 'bearer' is any person; the 'burden' is the mental and bodily complex of his living organism. The 'taking up,' the 'laying down,' of it are the one the exercise, the other the extinction, of *craving.* The simile is not so told as to convey what one would. expect, namely the laying down at death, the taking up at rebirth. But critics have written as if it did convey this: mind as well as body laid down at death, and a 'person' or ego left burdenless, or with a new burden. This is to garble the text.

Death is of the body only. The cessation in the dying instrument of the incorporeal processes or forces making up mind and their renewal by a new instrument could not—nay, cannot—be explained until the hour comes for man to learn—as he has not yet learned—what is the relation of mind to body. He was not ready to learn it then. He is still waiting and seeking for light, and Gotama either did not know, or did not go beyond the mandate of that inspiration that comes to great helpers of men.

What, then, is it that puzzles some inquirers in the Buddhist doctrine of rebirth? Buddhism, it is said, is illogical in order to serve an ethical purpose. It taught rebirth, that is life past and future, as well as present, to enforce the doctrine that good deeds done in past lives have brought happiness in this life, and that good deeds done in this life will bring happiness in a future life; that bad deeds have had, will have, the opposite effect. But at the same time it taught a doctrine of *an-atta.* Its teachers denied a self or soul, coming over from a past life into this life, or going from this life to another life in a new body. Now if I myself have not so passed on, will not so pass on, how have 'I' incurred, how shall 'I' incur, happiness or suffering because of what 'I' have done? This is the puzzle. It was put to Gotama himself, and answered in a peculiar and to us very baffling way.[8]

Let me recall the four ways[9] in which this difficulty arose then, and now arises. I said: *(a)* By an unfortunate ambiguity of language. The Buddhist word for life, in the sense of a span of individual life, was self-state *(atta-bhāva).* And the reflexive pronouns—myself, thyself, ourselves, etc.—were one and all expressed by the one word *atta-* in its various inflexions without any possessive pronoun attached to it. But *atta-* did not only mean our fairly unambiguous word [my-] self, [your-] self. *Attan,* in Sanskrit *ātman,* meant also spirit (derived, like
spirit, from breath); nay, it meant Divine Spirit, and was equivalent to Brahmạn. And these two were identified, not with anyone god of the ancient Indian pantheon, but with that deeper quest of the Indian mind after the source, essence, and world-will of the all. The Greek *pneuma* is the only word that approaches *ātman* in meaning; both are etymologically the same. Hence arose an ambiguity in

language into which we can hardly enter. If every time we use the word 'self,' we *might* mean 'Holy Spirit,' it is plain that the way to a wrong doctrine would lie perilously near. *Pneuma ho theos:* "God is spirit," said St. John. But Jesus, when he said, "My soul is exceeding sorrowful, even unto death," did not have to say *'the pneuma.'* He said, 'my *psyché,'* or its Aramaic equivalent. And when he was tempted—"If thou be the Son of God, cast *thyself* down"—he had not to say, in telling his experience, 'cast holy-spirit down,' but *'bale seauton katō.'* But in Pali, 'spirit,' , soul,' 'thyself,' would all three be *atta.* Thus it was but a little way for the Indian in Gotama's world to see in self or soul something mysteriously divine, though it is a much longer way for us.

(b) That little way had been travelled when Gotama lived. To the eye of mystic insight man's self *was* the divine self, dwelling in every man's heart, a small delicate replica of himself, body and mind, quitting the earth-body in sleep and at death. And as God it was eternal, unchanging, not subject to suffering or sorrow. For such was the essence of divinity.

Against this belief the Buddha at the outset of his career *(Vinaya,* i. 13) uttered an emphatic protest, a protest repeated, in part, throughout the Suttas. The argument he used is *only intelligible* when we see, in his repudiation of *atta-,* a self that is not human only, but also divine. It is not a denial of self or soul, but only of a theory of it *(atta-vāda).* In direct opposition to the teaching of those who said: *Tat tvam asi:* "That thou art; that Ātman is thyself; thou thyself art God," he said: "That is not thine, that art thou not, that is not thy God."

He would not have taken just this stand had he lived here and taught to-day. He would have agreed with us that self or soul, whatever else we mean by 'me,' is nothing divinely perfect, powerful, immutable, not susceptible of growth, but is a frail, fallible, mutable being, often suffering, capable of growth as of falling backward.

This did not exhaust Gotama's quarrel with *atta*-theory.

His other quarrel may be said to have been with the word itself. He was no materialist in the agnostic gospel he preached. But he saw that for people *words, names* too much meant *things (Dialogues of the Buddha,* i. 263; *Kindred Sayings,* i. 16, 18). Especially things they saw, touched. Even if they could not see or touch, to name a thing gave it substance in their notion of it. He waved aside metaphysical discussion with those who asked questions on metaphysic. And he had no scientific vocabulary to help out his meaning by physical analogies. But ever is he denying that 'body,' or 'mind,' or divine *ātman* is the real being of me that 'goes on, runs on' from birth to birth, like a force manifesting itself in materia] substance, or in modes of mind. It may be he wished to say: "If 'I know,' there *is* not a knower, not a knowledge: I am knowing, I am knowledge. If 'I love,' I do not have love. I am the loving, I am love. Give names, but do not lose sight of this, that a name may not correspond to a truth." But *he did not say this.* Let us not put words into his mouth. What he said was: *man goes on* (from life to life). And: man is neither body nor mind *(Saṃyutta,* iii. 33, 166), neither the name nor the thing. He did not say what is the very man. He probably did not know. He knew that 'the man' went on. 'He fares on, he runs on' *(saṃsarati, sandhāvati),* he said, from an unknown beginning *(ibid.* ii. 178, etc.). And so long as there is 'ignorance' and 'craving,' mind finds ever a new 'station.' *(ibid.* ii. 38, etc.). This 'mind' is not at each birth a new 'thing.' It is a causal process *(ibid.* ii. 20, 23; *Majjhima,* i. 259 f.).

(c) When, long after him, the mind of Pundits, or as we should say Scholastics, had been concentrating on the records called Vinaya and Dhamma, and when its somewhat crude analyses and dialectic termed Abhidhamma had been compiled, and when all three collections had been written down, the religious outlook was changing. The older Ātmanism had blended into what came to be called Bhaktism. The blending may be seen in the *Bhagavadgītā. Attan* as 'divine spirit' is no longer a danger-point in Buddhism,

neither in the *Milinda,* nor in the *Visuddhi Magga.* It is only the self as an entity apart from its functioning that has still to be contended with. So much does this negating it as such take up the attention of early and later Abhidhamma, that any positive, constructive thought on the subject is far too much neglected. And hence we of to-day are left often puzzling.

The Buddhist 'Fathers' were no more able than was their great master to say what man really is. But when, whether in the *Kathāvatthu* or in the *Milinda,* a 'going on from one world to another' is apparently denied, it is as much a denial as to *what* passes on as that there is a passing on. It is no transition of an identical, unchanging entity corresponding to the identical, unchanging label 'person,' 'being,' 'soul.' That there is a transition conceived is evident from the simile in the *Visuddhi Magga.* "As a man might cross a ditch by swinging himself as he hangs to a rope from a tree on this bank, so does mind *(viññāṇa)* at death proceed onward in causal relation to objects and so on" *(Visuddhi Magga,* p. 554). But though Buddhaghosa's language is copious (and often terribly involved), his rang of ideas is very small; those of the *Milinda* are smaller, those of the *Kathāvatthu* (I. 1) smallest of all. And why? Because their knowledge of natural laws and natural forces was so restricted and crude. They had some skill in dialectic, but not much else. There is a great gulf between them and us. They fought hard to beat down this notion of their 'man in the street': that when he *says* 'person,' 'being,' 'soul,' 'I,' 'you,' he *thinks* the word corresponds to a certain inner invisible objectified unity underneath the visible appearance. So hard did they fight that they lost sight of what was much more important: that the mind and body, into which they resolved man, were but instruments; that through mind and a series of bodies the indisputably real man expressed himself. The Buddhist Fathers have played a little into the hands of materialists

(d, e) For just as bell-push, fiery coil, and battery are not electric force, so is our tangible, visible, audible framework

not we, nor the 'mind' operating it either. But give me a body and I can express myself through it as what I am 'pleased to call my mind.' Hence it follows that all we need ask of any creed that teaches rebirth or survival is: How about the new body? We can leave the question of 'new' mind. Find man a new body, and he will work it with mind. *How* we cannot say till the relation of mind to body in general is understood.

When shall we see scientific attention—in psychology, biology, physics—waking up to concentrate on this wonderful and pressing problem—the new body that man, passing on, will work by mind? The so-called 'new psychologies' have not come to it yet, though they are so much prolegomenon to the great move on that is coming.[10] The psychology of to-day tries to build up the mind of the individual from the racial mind of the past. It has to deal in masses, for it had not the Buddhist secret of rebirth. The psychology of to-morrow will investigate the past of the individual—the last little bit of that past; and it will find itself up against the Buddhist doctrine of rebirth. The next step will be to inquire into the psychology of our future—into what *we* rise up as, when *we* discard this body, the whence of that new body and the nature of it. It is no idle quest, but of tremendous practical importance. Few of us will urgently need to wireless to the Antipodes, much less to Mars. But we all die, and very soon. Are we always going to be so childish as to be content, not only with creeds, but with sciences that leave us in ignorance of death, and so in the fear of death? This is no hopelessly impossible quest. Quietly research is going on, experiences are mounting up recorded more carefully now than ever. It is only the switching on of competent scientific investigation to an adequate extent and intensity that is lacking. This would in no long time bring us from our present darkness of fear and doubt and ignorance and anguish into a clearer air.

References

1. Brahma-world, *Questions of King Milinda,* i. 126.
2. *Saṃyutta,* ii. 236; *Aṅguttara,* i. 88; *Dhammapada,* 268; *Therīgāthā,* 153. etc.
3. *Kayassa bhedo. Bhedo* is etymologically 'breakege,' but it is chiefly used figuratively, as 'schism,' and in grammar, etc.
4. *Kindred Sayings,* i. 79 f.
5. *Dialogues of the Buddha,* iii. 17
6. *Iti-vuttaka,* § 83.
7. Above, p. 62.
8. See my *Buddhism* (Home University Library), pp. 138f.
9. Cf. above, p. 244 (4).
10. I hailed with pleasure the conclusion of Dr. Bernard Hollander's *In Search of the Soul* (London, 1921): "Instead of saying 'man has a soul,' it would be more correct to say 'man himself is a soul.'"

12

Some Psychological Points in the Kathā-Vatthu

Here and there in the foregoing pages allusion was made to certain works in process of being edited. Of these, during the past nine years (1914–23) the following first editions have been published by the Pali Text Society:

1. *Points of Controversy*, a translation of the *Kathā-Vatthu*, fifth book of the Abhidhamma-Piṭaka (cf. above, p. 158 f.). By S.Z. Aung and the writer. 1915.

2. The remainder of the *Paṭṭhāna* and its Commentary, seventh book of the Abhidhamma-Piṭaka (cf. above, pp. 135, 194). Edited by the writer. 1921–23.

3. The Commentary on the *Vibhanga*, second book of the Abhidhamma-Piṭaka, entitled *Sammoha-Vinodanī* ('Dispeller of Confusion,' cf. above, pp. 50, 185). Edited by A.P. Buddhadatta, Thera. 1923.

4. *The Visuddlti-Magga* (cf. above, p. 178 and *passim*). Edited by the writer. 1920, 1921.

5. A translation of No. 4, entitled *The Path of Purity*, by P. Maung Tin. Part I. 1923. The remainder will shortly be published.

6. A translation of the *Puggala-Paññatti*, fourth book of the Abhidhamma-Piṭaka, entitled *Designation of Human-Types*. By Bimala C. Law. 1924.

7. A translation of the first twenty-one of the fifty-six collections known as *Saṃyutta-Nikāya*, third of the Four

Nikāyas, entitled *Kindred Sayings,* i., ii. (Cf. abbve, p. 14 and *passim)* By the writer. 1917, 1922. Mr. F.L. Woodward is at work on the remaining thirty-five.

The translation of the concluding section of the First or Long-Sutta Nikāya *(Dīgha)* was published in 1921. (Cf. Bibliography.) And the near advent of that desideratum, a full English translation of the *Majjhima,* or Second Nikāya, is probable.

Much has been done. Much remains to be done—but not much more. The literature, ancient and mediaeval, is a limited field. By the middle of this century the harvesting of it should be as complete as is that of Vedic literature.

Before that date itw ill have become relatively easy to supersede this little provisional treatise by a worthier work. To aid my younger successor, whoever she or he nlay be, I would point out a few of the allusions of psychological interest occurring in the *Points of Controversy.*

(a) Consciousness, conceived as *(α)* acts of *minding* or awareness, and (*β*) co-efficients or adjuncts, some constant, some contingent, called 'mentals ' *(chetasikā,* cf. above, pp. 6, 8, 175), is a point of view that has prevailed in Theravāda Buddhism to the present day. Nevertheless, we note that the validity of such a classification was once a controverted point. If there were 'mentals' of *chitta,* why not make out 'contactals' as adjuncts of contact *(phassa)? (Points,* p. 197) With this too we may class the arguments *(a)* on the unmorality of the *sensus communis: mano,* and of its objects: *dhammas, as such* (p. 280), and *(b)* on insight and on memory or mindfulness (the more general concept), when no objects of the senses are present to, render them liable to moral stain (p. 236).

Here, as is the case in much pre-scientific dialectic, the weak analogies of language are oftener referred to than the facts of living experience.

(b) In connection with the process of cognition the *Points* make use repeatedly of a sequence which we do not find elsewhere (so far as I know): "adverting, ideating, co-

ordinated application, attending,[1] willing, anticipating, aiming" (*e.g.* pp. 221, 233, 237, 241, 244, 267, 307 f., 339, etc.).[2] It may possibly not imply sequence.

(*c*) The duration of a *chitta*-unit, referred to in my pages (pp. 14, 195), was clearly a controverted point. The weak analogy-logic again appears in the attempt to harmonize mind with life and cosmic process. The scriptures spoke of a threefold unit of duration: the nascent, the static, the evanescent. Was not the unit 'morning-noon-evening' such a unit? Could not mind-process be made to fit into that? Was it really so momentary a unit? Did devas in the immaterial sphere of mind *(arūpa)* only live there for a mind-instant? They had no bodies with the longer duration of youth, maturity, and old age as vehicles for the succession of innumerable mental flash-points.

(*d*) The perdurance of past consciousness too was a problem (p. 90). How could the remembered past persist in present consciousness?

(*e*) Regarding the interesting term *bhavanga*—it does not, I think, occur in the Kathā-vatthu. Its only appearance in the Piṭakas, except once where it is catalogued, in the Fourth Nikāya, as meaning just personality *(attabhāva)*, is in the Paṭṭhāna. This book, I have ventured to suggest elsewhere,[3] and its predecessor, the Yamaka, are later additions to the Abhidhamma-Piṭaka. The Kathā-vatthu is not the latest book, else it had ranked as No. 7, not No. 5. When the Paṭṭhāna was compiled, *bhavanga* had come into use as a psycho-physical term. The Kathā-vatthu arguments show a familiarity with some of the twenty-four relation's[4] *(paccayā*—the theme of the Paṭṭhāna), but they are not termed *paccayā,* nor is any passage cited from the work in connection with them. Had *bhavanga* been in use when the Kathā-vatthu was compiled, it would almost surely *not have been left to the Commentary* to use it in explaining the section where it is needed (p. 243). But this is merely I suggested, not in any way maintained as certain.

It was certain that such a term would come to be needed.

The Sāsana paid early and assiduous attention to attention. And for this reason: consciousness, awareness, only arose when a stimulus arose (see above, p. 15). What then was mind, where, how was it, when, as in sleep, or latent awareness, no cause was arousing it, calling it into actuality? Was it a sort of potential being, one with the life-flux? There were no words for the subconscious, the subliminal, the potential. In the Kathā-vatthu we see in this and that discussion the need of all three terms, albeit the need is not felt as such. We even see the need of our newer term 'fore-conscious.' Namely, in a controversy on the forms of bias, or latent tendencies *(anusaya)* in man *(Points,* p. 253 f., cf. p. 234): were these, as *latent,* unmoral, and only immoral when *patent?* Where the word 'potential' seemed needed, we have used it guardedly (p. 242), and only, I think, in translating the Commentary. The Commentator is trying, like a good chairman, to help out matters in the discussion. Do we actually possess past consciousness, or is it perished? A man, it explains, may be *samannāgata* (endowed with, possessed of); again, he may have *paṭilābha,* an actual equisition (of consciousness).

We know that we owe our articulate superiority here to Aristotle's distinction: *δυναμεῖ* and *ε'νεργεῖα.* And Buddhism ad not the good fortune to have an Aristotle. But Buddhism did, in response to a growth in its psychology, bring out and make function the word *bhavanga.* It is stamped significantly with the mark of a conviction in that 'coming-to-be' *(bhava),* which replaces for Buddhists the static conception of *atthitā* (being). We too are coming to be in need of a parallel term in English diction. We have dropped our Saxon *weorpan;* we have degraded our weaker word 'becoming.' When will the dynamic standpoint of our advanced thinking have so bitten into our outlook that we shall reinstate the fine old term in some modernized form?

(f) Concerning external perceptions there is the interesting passage (p. 193) as to whether we see space?[5] Buddhaghosa

is here anticipated (see above, p. 185); his more specific point is that we cannot say we 'see' long or short as we see colours. That sight is educated as to magnitude and much else by touch, that our seen magnitudes of three dimensions are visual interpretations of experience gained by hand and foot explorations is a very modern conclusion. The Theravada position is that we see not space, but the visible objects *(rūpāni)* filling space. Even these he will not admit to be anything but so many coloured areas. As solids they would be tangibles *(phoṭṭhabbāni.)* The question whether space is an element, but inaccessible to sense, he does not raise. Space is reckoned as a fifth or sixth element in both the Suttas and the Abhidhamma-Piṭaka.[6] The dissatisfied controverter—he is of the Andhaka school—maintains that we do 'see' intervals between objects, not as other objects, but as space. The Commentary supplies the explanation that we do not literally see, but are aware of the interval by *mano.* The comment is of interest, but might easily have been improved upon. Why is the work of *mano* here not called *takka:* logical inference? It occurs in the sacrosanct Suttanta: "So far as anything can be ascertained by *takka,* thou hast ascertained it."[7] And Buddhaghosa's comment is that the mode of *takka* here would be *anumāna:* inference (a later term). But it is over the function of *mano,* as my book has perhaps made clear, that Buddhist psychology leaves much to be desired. (Nor was Aristotle for that matter, any better.[8]) Thus: the objects of their sixth sense—*sensus communis* I have called it—of *mano* were *dhammā,* or as we might say presentations, or, with Hume, impressions and ideas. Further, this sixth sense, figured as gate or door, received and co-ordinated all the more elementary, the simpler objects of the five senses. Hence the objects of *mano* are by the Buddhist books (and from the first) shown to be complex. But *ākāsa-dhātu,* the element of space, is a simple object.[9] Yet we read nowhere any intelligent discussion on this dual capacity of *mano* both to apprehend the simple and to co-ordinate simple impressions into complexes or percepts.

There is more matter of psychological interest in the Kathāvatthu, but in the foregoing points only can we say that the subject is not merely touched, but just a little scratched. If the readers will consult the analytical table pp. xviii to xxvii (in our translation), they will see that such questions were raised by all the eighteen schools. But chiefly, on the whole, by the various subdivisions together known as the Andhakas (see plate, p. xxix) of South-East India *(ib.*, p. xliii). The orthodox or Theravāda attitude in these matters is by no means always the more intelligently alert or convincing. It could hardly fail to be otherwise. To be orthodox usually implies being *that which has done with growing.*

That the amount of inquisitive alertness revealed in the past by heterodox schools led to no more fruitful results than we have on record is also not surprising. These early psychologizers had inherited a certain positive body of data due to observation of mental procedure. But in their controversies we seldom if ever find that their intelligence has learnt this lesson: what was got was due to the mental alertness exercised by the man, or the men 'who saw' *(chakkhurnanto)* about *the things we find.* If we are to get further, we must not only argue from these data; we must get more data, and in the same way. We too must observe and see. We must compare; we must measure; we must record the results. They were not yet an old Church, but already theirs was the backward view: "Is it not said in the Suttanta? Was it not said by the Exalted One ?"

Poor Exalted One, most lovable and very wise, with his: "Be ye your own refuges! Have resort to yourselves! The Way is clearly taught. Walk ye in it, for Way means progress, Way means growth, Way means 'leaving the things that are behind.' Ye *are* not, nor are ye *not;* ye are becoming, ye are children of the world's *Werden."*

What, for that matter, is our psychology, what is our philosophy doing with their own too backward vision, to warrant us in correcting the Budhists?

References

1. If this list is really a living sequence, "attention" (manasikāra) must here be = apperception (*javana*).
2. In the Index, *s.v.* Adverting, p. 272 should be deleted, and these references added. The term is in the *Milinda* (cf. above, 157), but not the sequence.
3. *J.P.T.S.*, 1920–23, p. 56.
4. *Points*, pp. 182, 294.
5. See my Introduction, *Points*, p. liv.
6. *Digha*, iii. 247; *Majjhima*, i. 423, iii, 31; *Aṅguttara* i. 176; *Dhammasaṅgaṇi* § 638.
7. *Saṃyutta*, i. 55; *Kindred Sayings*, i. 80.
8. See the writer's *Will to Peace*, 1923, p. 63 f.
9. *Points*, 192.

13

Development of the Anti-Soul Attitude

And finally a parting word.

The attempt has been made in these pages to show how far the teaching of Theravāda Buddhism included what we now call principles of psychology; and further, that such psychology as there was grew. What made it grow as it did, what stimulated and what hindered its growth is not discussed.[1] But allusion has been made to this, that in developing some point of doctrine here or there, the later teaching becomes all but discrepant with the utterances on that point which we judge to be earliest in the records.

The quasi-discrepancy may take the form of a positive dogma in the later books, concerning a non-positive, a veiled teaching in the earlier utterances. For instance, there is a positive teaching that 'the heart' is the 'seat' of 'thinking, replacing the guarded term 'that rūpa which is the base of thinking,' etc. (p. 71). Professor Stcherbatzky inclines to think that 'heart-base' was a metaphysical datum and not the bodily organ.[2] But when in a work nearly (?) of Vasubandhu's date—the Nidāna-kathā—we find a man's thinking referred to his heart's flesh (*gadayamaṃsa*)[3] we can scarcely agree that the average Buddhist culture was so subtle.

Or the discrepancy may be sharper. For instance, it has been shown, (pp. 254,265 f.) that where the founder is recorded as saying that all men 'fare on, run on' from one world to another, later records say positively 'no being so fares on.' The identical person does not, else he would appear as necessarily a king or a serf in his next rebirth:[4]—a curiously slovenly way of confusing the man with his earth-body and his other earthly conditions. A still later teaching explained that there were conventions in popular speech not valid for the wise man when considering things in their ultimately real nature *(param'attha)*.[5] A teacher of the multitude would use the conventions *(sammuti-kathā)*, but with a 'closed fist' as to ultimates.

Now *this distinction is not clearly applied* in the Kathāvatthu just where it is needed, namely, where the opponent says: Did not the Master teach about this and that *puggala?* The nearest we get to it is earlier in the Sutta discourses, where a warning is uttered against the fetter of words, of names.[6] But the distinction as a doctrine is clearly a development later than those in vogue when the Council of Patna brought about the compilation of the Kathā Vatthu. Else it had surely been used.

Let the reader bear in mind these typical cases of what we may call the more-wording of a simpler, older pioneer teaching, when he comes across such sweeping assertions as that Gotama taught we have no souls, we have no 'we.' We have rather to consider, unfortunately, not what did he say? but what is he made to say, and by whom? or at what period in the history of the doctrine is he made to say it? What is he recorded to have first put forward as his message? What are recorded as his last injunctions? And how long after him was his teaching *and* the 'more-wording' of his church set down?"

For the Pali literature which is recognized as embodying the authoritative teaching of Theravāda Buddhism is not one compact system evolved in some brief Elizabethan florescence. It is a series, or rather a string, of detached units and groups of units, widely detached for the most part in time and in place. It contains in many units much patchwork of juxtaposed fragments and a great deal of quite obvious 'editing.' Between its earliest books and the still standard manual of *The Compendium* lie about fifteen centuries. Truly has there been time enough for development and also for decay! We have only to compare, say, our Bede and Caedmon with Donne, both as to their range and form of diction, as to their pen-skill and as to their development in ideas.

But in claiming a development in the Sāsana of just this dogma of An-atta (non-soul, non-spirit, non-self), we want to get beyond the Venerable Bedes of Buddhism. Can we possibly discern what was the attitude of the founder? Did he start his mission with such a dogm ? Did he end it with such? Did he himself develop his teaching with respect to it? For a gospel is likely to be in a more fluid state during the first months of its being launched than when it has got a footing. An infant church has much to learn at its first inauguration. Its leader has even more to learn by his first contact, as teacher, with all sorts and conditions of men and traditions.

A young idealist, his character based on desire to help his little world, driven by an urge to bring them a message of help, he may elaborate in solitary pondering a theme he judges is needed. When he is confronted with men and women and children, the message he is moved to say may be quite other than what he had planned. Thus Gotama shrank from uttering what he had planned in wrestling for light. When he first uttered his message it was of a different import from that. He spoke of the Way of godly living,[7] of holiness as being our very best in mind, word, and deed. He spoke of this as a Middle Way. His Bo-tree record tells nothing of this.

But almost at once he is brought up against the opinions taught and discussed in his day. Not about the gods. The great gods seem to have been of a past day. But up against the Spirit (Ātman) held to dwell in—nay, to be the soul in—the body; and up against the Fire, also an embodiment of the Godhead. Gotama was intent, from first to last, far more on what his fellows did and should or should not do than on what they ultimately were. He was not from first to last a teacher, much less an inquirer into the whole nature of man. He gave what he could with open hand; he said so.[8]

But he had never undergone the long training of brahmins, and he was wise enough to know that they could not give the help he was yearning to give, and that his age knew profoundly little. His silences to questioners are famous. If he gave all, he can have had nothing to hold back.

Nevertheless, he had to take up an attitude towards other men's teachings, even if the matters dogmatized about seemed to him of relatively less importance. He sought mainly to lighten sorrow and suffering. He is made to say so with great emphasis. He held that the way out to more happiness was a moral religion. Sacrifice and ritual, priest and unmoral gods to be propitiated—these had begun to crumble. For the average mind, conduct was swayed by the alternatives of self-indulgence and asceticism; for the more thoughtful, there was the danger of complacently identifying the ego with the very Brahman, divine well-spring of creative power, eternal, immutable blessedness. That the Way he taught might be the long, long way of Brahma-will working in man's will he saw not. Who did? He saw only the static Brahman or Ātman, not the moving Will. And how could this frail transient body or mind in any way be the eternal, the immutable God-Self? If either were It, man could say, I will be powerful, beautiful, eternal, and all the rest. There was one's reason here in protest, even if there were no piety to be hurt, no humility to be shocked. This protest, that man's 'self' is neither body nor mind, and, for the reasons given, forms what is apparently the simple genuine nucleus of the much 'edited' second sermon.[9] There is not a word that man *is not attā.*[10] His first sermon to a group of the laity who had not come to hear the new recluse teach, but asked, in passing, had he seen a woman of the town pass by, was on the text: 'Is it not better to seek the self than such an one?' But we cannot tell, from the ambiguity in diction of which I have written (p. 261 f.), whether he meant 'seek Brahman,' or 'seek yourselves.' We do know that the records make him teach the taming of the self time and again. Was it not part of the best life to win self-mastery? And we can almost hear him protesting, 'How can I, who taught man to tame the self, and then to rely upon it, be said to deny it ?'

Among his many parables is one that, so far from denying that man is more than body and mind, actually *implies* that he is chiefly and centrally soul or self—that he is *'he.'* It occurs repeatedly. ' If you saw folk carrying away faggots, brushwood, leaves, from this Jeta Grove and burning it, would you say they are carrying away the grove? . . . Even so, put aside what is not you, what is not of you, your body, your mental faculties.'[11]

There is an incident related which betrays how very far was Gotama from readiness to speak dognlatically on man as being a soul, or not soul. He met the repeated inquiry of Vacchagotta: 'Is there or is there not an Attā?' with silence. Asked by Ānanda why he was silent, he replied: 'If I said there is, he would figure it as mmutably eternal; if I said there is not, he would think he perishes utterly at death. Or, he would say, is it consistent with your teaching: no *dhammas* are *attā?* or he would think: then *I* was *attā,* but am now so no longer.'[12] This episode may or may not be Church-edited. But in either case it throws into clearest light one point. and that is, that no unprejudiced reader could say the denial of self or soul is a central tenet of this teacher's gospel! That, having such a tenet, he should have been silent, if the questioner were not a wise person, is credible, albeit improbable, for might not the man's salvation depend on his conversion to the 'right view'? But that he should comment *afterwards': 'If* I said, Soul is'; *'if* I said, Soul is not,' as if the matter were merely speculative, is utterly incredible, if he held it of any importance that he should be known as a teacher of No-soul. Yet Buddhists of to-day incline to hold that Anatta is a central tenet, and consider the opposite belief a very 'pernicious' creed!

When we come to Gotama's parting words, we should be prepared to find some precious survivals of his real sayings. As a pioneer he had come forward with some startling sayings. Very few, however, would be remembered. He was unknown. He had no recorders. His hearers never dreamt of the wondrous future of his teaching. As an aged, dying teacher, deeply revered and beloved by his little world, his last words would have weight and be branded on the memory of ear-witnesses in this and that poignantly impressive interview. The long Sutta of the Utter Passing Away is, as a whole, a curious patchwork. The numbered formulas are there as usual, and very clumsily sewn on.[13] But we certainly discern a more intimate actuality, a very human note, in some of this noble friend's sayings.

Do we then find him urging his disciples to hold fast and foremost the negation: all things, all men, are *an-attā?* There is not one word recorded on the subject. To them, sorrowful, he utters the oft-taught reminder: all things are transient *(anicchа)*. And this implies, of course, a ruling out of the mistaken belief in the self being a very God within, unchanging, almighty. But this would never then and there, at his passing, have been left implicit, if the rejection of that self had been his real teaching.

What do we get? That a church's test of genuine unworldliness *(sāmuññā)* is to be walking in the (eightfold) way of the best living. So saying, he was bringing in *his last convert.* Again, 'Why have you and I needed to wander so very long from birth to birth? Because we have not understood the real cause of sorrow and how to do away with the cause.'[14] Note here the personal emphasis 'you and I.' He was speaking of the wood, not of the faggots. Yet he was speaking to disciples, not to worldlings. *We* have been going from birth to birth. There has not been a breaking up and somehow a reforming of all that is we. 'The same emphasis, the same silence in another last address.[15]

And what in those last addresses was he mainly urging on his little village-churches? Mainly his life's message—virtue and holiness. *Sīla,* the moral life; *samādhi,* training of self, or of *chitta; paññā,* insight that makes-to-become; *vimutti,* freedom from whatever acts as a drawback to holiness. This, worded alas! only in the usual formula, is recorded as his constant theme on the whole of that last wearily-walked tour.[16]

There is just one passage where *anatta* is mentioned. It is in a numbered category.

Asked concerning the chances of the Vajjian federation in any war with Kosala and Magadha, he named certain social conditions making for national strength. Thereafter he took up these as a sermon modified to suit the religious. Five versions are given as five successive variants on the text. Then a sixth of fewer heads. And, remembering the mode of recording his sayings, and the length of time, and noting the editorial diction, we are convinced, if no tradition is fettering us, that we can put these variants on one side as *relatively* very poor evidence that he uttered them.

Let us now place in close juxtaposition to these logia a passage from Buddhaghosa's *Visuddhi Magga,* the approximate date usually assigned to that work being AD 420: 'Wherefore the men of old[17] said: There is no doer of the deed, nor experiencer of the result; bare states *(dhammā)* proceed (or occur)—this is the right view. . . . Of life's way *(saṃsāra)* there is no maker, deva or God: bare states proceed caused by a collection of conditions.'[18] No doer, only doing.

Much water had flowed down Ganges to the sea between such utterances (they could be multiplied) and those of the Suttas, even if the Suttas do not for the most part give us the real logia of the founder. The negating, the atheistic emphasis has become sharper. And it is more a-psychic. In the Suttas the Ātman (Brahman) and man's self are not so clearly distinguished. It is said '(Whatever else you ultimately are,) *you* are neither body nor mind. But put away these opinions as to what self really is.' In the long and larger traditional cult to which Buddhaghosa was heir, the Ātman as mmanent godhead no longer menaced. One would think he might have cultivated a modified theory of man's nature as that 'self' which his great Master had bidden his followers first tame and then depend upon. But, to quote a Teuton proverb, his teachers had emptied out the baby with the bath. Together with Ātmanism, they had ejected the human wielder of mind and body, the very psyche or self who plays on those instruments.

And so firmly established has this atheistic, a-psychic dogma become, that Buddhaghosa, while asserting it in many ways and contexts, does not judge it necessary to argue; he just affirms, or rather he just reiterates denial.

Going back to Milinda, we find no Porāṇa sanction cited, but a similar a-psychic position. Here there is no atheistic stress, and there is an attempt to argue in maintaining the negation. A psyche would need no apparatus of sense.[19] The reasoning is very inadequate and restricted. Psychic life is considered only from the receptive point of view. Reaction, the will are ignored. Would the psyche require no apparatus to act? Would she require a body to be visible, to speak, to write books, to make music?

Going back again, we come to the Abhidhamma. It is some interval—would that we knew how long!—for there is all the difference possible between the easy, often graceful, pen-manship in the shallow analogies of the Milinda and the rigid attempts at dialectic in the Kathāvatthu. And there is this other notable difference: Nāgasena dismisses the questions on *jīva* and *vedagū* lightly enough. But the first, the only lengthy, the only really belaboured point of controversy in the Kathāvatthu is that with the Puggalavādins, in or out of the Sāsana: that a self or soul, now called *puggălă,* not *attā,* is 'known' or found.

Clearly we are now at a stage of development in the Anatta doctrine where, so far from being a central doctrine, it was not even accepted by all of the Sangha or Sāsana. It is having, we may say, to fight for its life. Those who would not accept thorough-going negation of a self-unity were Vajjian brethren—associated with dissent in the past[20]—and Sammitiyas, so the (later) Comentary tells. Later they joined the Mahā-Sanghikas. We learn from Vasubandhu[21] that, during any one life-span, a human being was not merely a verbal unity, a 'man' so called, nor merely a thinkable or logical unity; he was a veritable entity *for the time being*. Hence we have here an extension of a Theravāḍa theory, namely, that something ultimately real, an irreducible element, may have the transient nature of a derivative compound, or, as we say, of a phenomenon, for a given time-interval only.

We come back finally to the two older bodies of 'sayings,' some portions of which, it is alleged, were fixed in some sort of canonical form and 'chanted' in chorus at the first Council.[21] Here we are somewhat nearer in time to the inception of the church of those whom their little world called, not Buddhists, but Sakyans, or Sakya-sons, and whose founder was spoken of among men as 'the recluse Gotama.' But we are still a long way off. We have, as we all know, documents before us which for centuries were not written, but had existence only in huiman memories—or perhaps very nearly so. And more, they betray the marks of addition, both of external addition and also of internal interpolation. And more, for the most part they are records, not of the natural way of human speech, but of that speech reset in artificial diction, so as to aid oral transmission; such as metrical diction, and refrains, both in narrative, in statements of doctrine (formulas), and in exposition of the same. I hazard the judgment that the refrains were the work of some zealous organizer Moggalī-putta-Tissa probably—after the Patna Council had closed the Canon as to Vinaya and Dhamma.

And what did these editors find and hand on about *anatta*?

With the Sāsana-cult become paramount, the brahmin Ātman-cult had been for the time suppressed. The ambiguous word *atta* would no longer call up a concept of an immanent Deity. The Master and the 'great Theras,' it was thought, must have meant the human unity we mean when, with nearly every sentence, we speak of 'I,' 'mine,' 'thou,' 'we,' and the like, This must be the attā whom it is illogical to seek in body or mind, And so we get to fuller negations: all the world is *anattā;* all *dhammas* (things, or phenomena, or, according to mediaeval metaphysic, all ultimates) are anattā; all man is anattā. The terms 'all' and 'world,' it is true, are explained as all sense-experience. But their psychology scarcely sufficed to include a *caveat* that our sense-experience is very relative, and only brings us impressions by five limited gates,

Yet they were beginning, as the new state-church of the new empire, to annex the philosophical culture of the country. And such slender development of this as they acquired they used to establish a sceptical, mainly negative doctrine, not so much of anti-Ātmanism, as of a-psychism. It was one thing to say, as the founder probably did say: neither body nor mind is the Self. They are as the bundles of kindling to the grove. It was another thing to say: *'all things are without self [or soul.]'* Or—

> *'Being'? Why dost thou harp upon that word?*
> × × × × ×
> *This* a *mere bundle of formations is . . .*

and follow up this by holding up a parallel between two such radically incomparable terms as a chariot and a living human being.[22]

The latter passage, a sheet-anchor in argument to both Nāgasena and Buddhaghosa, is ascribed to a woman. Sister Vajirā. It is a priceless irony of history that Gotama should have foreseen the danger of admitting women to his Order, and that the danger should have lain, not in her disturbing concord or sensemastery, but in her leading around learned doctors by a semblance of logic!

This very slight sketch must end. We are scarcely yet in a position to estimate adequately what the Suttas really yield us as to this *anattā* attitude. A few of us know a little of their contents. Most of us, including most members of the Buddhist churches, lay and religious, know scarcely anything thereof. We and they are much like Christians into whose hands their Scriptures in the vernacular have not yet been placed. Some years hence, historical scholarship will know them from A to Z, and will discuss them critically, and not to minister to modern agnosticism, nor to sectarian defence or attack.

But scholarship will confirm this: that, in spite of much clerical asseveration of anattā, the word *atta-* both is, *and was,* ambiguous; that the meaning of the idea 'self, soul, being,' was fluctuating, confused, and not very consistently expressed; that the development in the way of negation is traceable; and that the ignorance of man's nature was a little more profound than it is anywhere to-day. It is a fairly safe inference, in estimating beliefs, that the saying of a 'view' very often, very loudly, very firmly, may be a substitute for clear or reasoned knowledge. It is certainly not easy, either in old or new discussion, to read any convincing reason why acceptance of truth in man as really soul, self, spirit, should be so 'pernicious.' That there was unsoundness in the once current Ātmanistic attitude is plausible. But it is not so easy to justify the condemnation of a-psychism in any but a materialistic doctrine. Buddhism was never that.

Even with more light of internal evidence we shall not know clearly what Gotama taught, so is he smothered. If we shall still find that, as is here affirmed, his church 'more-worded' his message, it is only what all churches have done. It is true that he lived and taught many years. Possibly he knew of, possibly he condoned, the method of re-wording by metrical and prose refrains. But still, what he seems to have been saying at the end was not the burden of much in the Suttas nor in their style. He was not saying: 'I am the greatest teacher in the world. I know all. All is anattā—you are not Spirit, not self. Be careful to teach the Dhamma in formulas.'

Neti, neti: not thus, not thus! They say he said this:

'I am a feeble old man in the eighties;[23] my body barely holds together, like a strapped cart. You have been very kind and good to me, but I leave you, for nothing lasts unchanging, and dear ones must part. Great is the moral life, great is self-training, great is wisdom's vision, great is liberty from bonds! Teach these things to men in this world and in the other world out of your loving compassion. And depend upon yourselves. Accomplish earnestly! You will attain the highest, they of you who are willing to learn.'[2]

References

1. For some of the internal conditions see the writer's 'A Milestone in Pali Text Society Work,' *J.P.T.S.*, 1923; 'The Abhidhamma Piṭaka and Commentaries,' *J.R.A.S.*, April, 1923; Preface to second edition *Buddhist Psychological Ethics*, 1923.
2. *Vasubandhu*, London, R.As. Soc., 1923, p. 18.
3. Fausböll, Jātaka, i. 25. Cf. Rhys David's *Buddhist Birth Stories, in loco*, new edition, London, 1924, Broadway Translation Series, entitled *The Story of the Lineage.*
4. *Kathāvatthu=Points of Controversy*, p. 28; cf. *Milinda*, i., pp. 111, 112, 120.
5. *Kathāvatthu Commentary*, cf. *Points*, p. 63; *Mil.* i. 226.
6. See above, pp. 32, 263. *Kindred Sayings*, i. 22.
7. *Brahma-chariya.* On the word see the writer's *Old Creeds and New Needs*, London, 1923, p. 77.
8. *Digha*, ii., p. 100.
9. Known as the Anattalakkhaṇa- sutta. *Vin.*, i. 100.
10. I deprecate the wording of my learned firiends Dr J. Estlin Charpenter, *Origins of Theistic Buddhism*, p. 20; 'Gotama sought . . . . by convincing them that they had no selves,' and Sir Charles Eliot, *Hinduism and Buddhism*, i. 185: 'He then explained to them that *there is no such thing* as self,' . . . . namely, in this sermon. *'Neither body nor mind is self'* is not quite coincident in import. Nor can it be clearly made out that any ethical teaching as to unselfishness is bound up with *anattā*. In altruism we are on more modern ground.
11. *Saṃyutta*, iii. 33 f.; iv. 82. This was suggested to me years ago by Sir Charles Eliot, but I was very blind.
12. *Saṃyutta*, iv. 398. Oldenberg discusses this, but with a different emphasis. *Buddha*, sixth edition, p. 313f.
13. *E.g.*, eight causes of earthquakes (evidently only minor seismic shivers were in memory), or the back-and-forth Jhānas of the death-bed (which the attendants could not possibly have known of), and some others. *Dialogues*, ii. 78 f.
14. *Dialogues*, ii. 96. Also in *S.B.E.*, xi., p.1f.
15. *Ibid.*, 131.
16. *Ibid.*, 85, 86, 89, 97, 100, 105, 132, 136
17. *Porāṇā.* Presumably the men who sponsored the newly-edited canon after the Third Council. Cf. my discussion, *Visuddhi Magga*, 'Afterword,' p. 764 f. (P.T.S. edition).

18. *Op. cit.*, p. 602 f. For other such passages translated see Warren's *Buddhism in Translations*, pp. 145. 241, etc.
19. See above, p. 163 f.
20. Stcherbatzky, *Vasubandhu* (R.A.S., 1923) pp. 25, 70.
21. *Vin., Text,* iii. (Chulla Vagga, XI).
22. Cf. 'appeals to authority,' *Points of Controversy,* p. 65 f. I have gone into this mater in *The Will to Peace,* London, 1923, p. 118.
23. *Asītiko* is not eighty, but eight-ish, octogenarian.
24. All of these sentens are in the concluding pages of the book of the Utter Passing Away (Mahā Parinibbāna Sutta).

Epilogue

This little book reumes its life with a patch-work *coda:* a few words of psychological additions; a few more of philosophy and of eschatology. These are not out of place in discussing the unspeeialized theorizing of the past. All of the historical sketches of which the book consists are a patchwork; or at best a few transverse sections in a tradition of centuries, along which, in one corner of the earth, human thought-wording is found trying 'earnestly to accomplish' vision into what men should be and do.

To attain this vision, it was necessary to look into what men actually were, as body, as mind, as self. But the primary quest of the Buddhist, as of his founder, always was: vision into what we ought to be and do.

If we turn to the world of Greek thought, we seem to find a greater, a more detached interest in the quest of what man, in the midst of the nature to which he is bound, *is.* What he should be and do followed from what he was. He was to live and act 'conformably to nature.'[1] As he emerged into a realization of himself as a world-knower and world-worder, the Greek was fascinated by the wonder of the senses and their world-pictures, and by mind as the mirror of these. And he was so much more of a mirror of them than a mover. His power over the external world was less than that of any child of our day. Hence his poverty of wording concerning his own impact upon the world, as compared with his thinking and his wording and (in art) his working concerning the impact of the world upon him.

Where the Buddhist exceeded his primary aim, he did

not get far, and when he strove to get further, he was prone to err and to stray from truth. He was alert as to the near way of the very gates of sense. And why? Because these were less inlets of knowledge than of obstruction and danger. They were to be 'guarded,' not for the joy and interest in the knowledge they brought, but lest the inpouring current they might become should overwhelm the little boat trying to cross the perilous seas of Saṃsāra.

But when Buddhists tried to penetrate within the gates of sense, they were without orderly vision. There was an inner central gate—a 'sixth sense' co-ordinating—and, independent of sense, a hotchpotch of faculties or states, some simple, some complex; among them a few more or less inter-identical *(paññā, vipassanā, abhisamaya paṭivedha)* instrmnents of the spiritual life. Taken with body, they all made up a congeries, a 'mere bundle.' Such was their 'man,' their 'I,' their 'self.' They cut off the well-spring of creative evolution. Their whole 'vision was but a transverse section just 'going on,' both microcosmic and macrocosmic. Even the goal of parinirvāṇa—the after-being of the perfected man at his last passing away—was but a mysterious vanishing from all possible worlds of rebirth into the void, worded only as a negation.

In a way they transcended the ignorance of their time and their world as to 'nature,' for they judged that nature to be teeming and moving and evolving from one cyclic cataclysm to new evolution and back again. They transcended the ignorance of their time and their world as to life, for they raised the vague faith in survival to a natural law of life as a series of rebirths and redyings in a long, long upward way of purgation. But the blind spot of the spirit of their time and their world, as to a well-spring and well-goal of life and of all things, was reflected in a wavering agnosticism about the inner well-spring who is the real man, and then in a dogmatic nihilism concerning any such well-spring using the instruments of body and mind.

Hence it may be that, with far better opportunities in the

way of materials to hand, we no more get a vision of *will* in Buddhist thought than we do in Greek thought. As the heirs of the latter and not of the former, we in the West have been taking a very long way round to come to a full realization of man's powers of reaction to, of impinging upon, the world which so constantly impinges upon him. We have not nearly come to it yet. But the outlook of the Buddhist on man as dynamic, as kinetic, was very favourable to remarkable inductions as to will, had he been capable of more worthily wording it.

Consider his materials: There was unquestionably a greater capacity for what is called *iddhi,* will-power, than there is now even in India, let alone the West. No one, save a materialist or a prejudiced sceptic, can study Buddhist literature and deny this. It is too cheap an evasion to write down all these thoughtful, sincere men as liars, as deluded all the time. Next, there was the faith in 'mind' *(chitta)* as infinitely ductile and plastic (pp. 19, 36 f.), and in the sense-apparatus as so many *indriyas*—that is, ruling or controlling things, faculties, not passive as mirrors, but engaged in clash and collision (pp. 63, 121, 166 f.). Next, there was the faith in the necessity of 'training the self' *(atta-dama),* however they conceived self (p. 37). Next, there was a keen sense of the importance of endeavour *(vāyāma)* and of energy *(viriya),* of effort *(padhāna-āyūhana),* together with a fourfold scheme of, 'Best Efforts' in self-mastery *(B.P.E.,* § 1366). Next there was the belief in life-experience as work *(karma)* bringing forth results which were a sequel themselves of work. Next, there was life conceived as process, and as a cause-determined process. And, lastly, the belief in life as a very long period and opportunity of becoming of growth—a rising on stepping stones of dead selves to higher things.

All of this is put forth here and there in a way that is quite explicit, in a way that, taken together, amounts to a world-dhamma, a view of things. But it is not in any way resumed and gripped as a view, ealized as such. It is not held together by any clue or keyword about man's nature, such as to-day we might call a philosophical, or a psychological principle. The Greeks and Buddhists laid hold, each of them, on a principle of natural causation. The Greeks applied it *to account for* serial order in the sense-pictures. The Buddhists applied it to teach how the series of sense-pictures and the resulting desires *might be shut off*. But neither Greek nor Buddhist was able to word a principle of will, nor of man as essentially a willer. The Greek's world-pictures developed into a concept of man as essentially and practically a static thinker. The Buddhist was too fluid altogether. For all his noble adumbrations of world-*werden,* of world-work, of training, of many lives rough-hewing man's will into holy living, he failed for lack of a vision of that will as the playing upon an instrument, and of man as the player.

It is for us of to-day and to-morrow, reading these things of the past and heeding their call to us to 'accomplish earnestly,' to work out a truer word than they had, a truer word than we yet have, of man and of will.